Mankind Man Unkind

Albert J. Myers

To order additional copies of this book, contact:
Xlibris Corporation
1-888-795-4274
www.Xlibris.com
Orders@Xlibris.com
95873

CONTENTS

SOUTH VIETNAM
1968

*(This map is provided as a reference point; it shows the locations of divisions in 1968.)

DMZ
Dong Ha • • Quang Tri
• Hiep (Camp Evans)

I CORPS

Da Nang •
• Hoi An

3rd Marine Division
1st Marine Division
1st Marine Air Wing
36th Tactical Fighter Wing
1st Bde, 5th Infantry Division
101st Airborne Division
XXIV Corps

American Division:
3rd Brigade of 4th Infantry Division
196th and 198th Light Infantry Bdes
11th Infantry Brigade
3rd Brigade of 1st Cavalry Division
(Airmobile) also attached

Chu Lai •

1st Brigade of 4th Infantry Division
Elements of 2nd Brigade, 4th Infantry Div.
Elements of 173rd Airborne Brigade
Elements of 1st Cavalry Division (Airmobile)
2nd Brigade of 4th Infantry Division
Elements of 25th Infantry Division
Elements of 1st Cavalry Division (Airmobile)
31st Tactical Fighter Wing
1st Field Force Headquarters
5th Special Forces Group Headquarters
Army Engineer Command
18th Engineer Brigade
12th Tactical Fighter Wing
483rd Troop Carrier Wing
35th Tactical Fighter Wing
Elements of 101st Airborne Division
Task Force South

II CORPS

• Dak To

An Khe •   Phu Cat •
• Pleiku
• Rok Valley

• Tuy Hoa
• Phu Hiep

• Ban Me Thuot

Nha Trang •

FISH HOOK
• Quan Loi   Cam Ranh Bay
Iron Triangle   Phan Rang •

PARROT'S BEAK
Cu Chi •   • Xuan Loc
      • Bien Hoa
Tan An • ★SAIGON   Phan Thiet •
      • Long Thinh
Dong Tam •   • Vung Tau
Rach Gia •   My Tho
Can Tho •
MEKONG DELTA

III CORPS

1st Infantry Division
11th Armored Cavalry Regiment
3rd Tactical Fighter Wing
1st Brigade of 101st Airborne Division
199th Light Infantry Brigade
Elements of 9th Infantry Division
25th Infantry Division
3rd Brigade, 82nd Airborne Division
U.S. Army, Vietnam
1st Logistical Command
1st Signal Brigade
1st Aviation Brigade
II Field Force
44th Medical Brigade
18th Military Police Brigade
20th Engineer Brigade
1st Air Cavalry Division (Airmobile)

CA MAU PENINSULA

IV CORPS

Elements of 9th Infantry Division
Delta Helicopter Aviation Battalion
Headquarters for Navy River Patrol Boats,
Seal Teams, Junk Forces; Army Special
Forces.

Vietnam has many stories as it had many participants and has many misconceptions as it had from nightly TV viewers. Vietnam War was no different than other wars. It too had its heroes and villains.

I was fortunate to come home from my tour in Vietnam. There I saw the best and the worst in men, mankind and man unkind to witness the tears of a man who had to kill rather than be killed. I saw a man who saved a biddy's life at the expense of his own. I saw the men and women responsible for building the Third Marine Division Memorial Children's Hospital at Dong Ha.

I could tell you about my medals or the things we accomplished in my tour, but the real story of Vietnam was revealed when we got home. For many, that's when the real war began. Our welcome home was not forthcoming. We were scattered about the country in hopes that we could assimilate into society despite the myth projected on the television, in the papers, and within the covers of neatly tucked magazines. Yes, contrary to all the TV shows and news stemming from Vietnam, the guys serving there were not all killers, village burners, or drug addicts. They were your brothers and fathers, sons, cousins and classmates, neighbors and friends.

America is finally opening its heart, mind, and arms to these brave men and women, but many still consider themselves the walking wounded and envy those who died in "Nam." They escaped the humiliation they have had to endure and say those who have their names inscribed on the Vietnam Veterans Memorial were the lucky ones.

For those who have died, we thank you for your sacrifice. America is still the home of the brave and the free. For those who have returned, your hardships will make you more understanding and sympathetic toward the sorrows of others. For those who are still fighting, may you find the peace of mind that eludes you.—Al Myers

Edited by JJ

Ours was the sunshine, a world of beach blankets and seagulls with silver wings flying overhead. To lie in that sun was to dream dreams of faraway places hidden in the clouds. There was no war here, just the feeling and the sharing, a world of our own, a world of love.

I remember her lying next to me. I remember exploring her body with my mind, my eyes, and my touch. I remember kissing her gently, brushing the tiny beads of perspiration above her lips, like the dew on lilies on an April morning.

"Don't ever leave me." I startled her with those words.

"I'll wait for you," she had replied, her eyes filling with tears, "I'll wait for you *forever.*" And then, like a sand castle dream erased by the sea, it was all gone.

"Gentlemen," crackled the voice over the cockpit loudspeaker, "you are now at Da Nang Air Base, Republic of South Vietnam. On behalf of the crew and all America, we wish you a safe and speedy return back home. Good luck."

Vietnam. My new world. As I stumbled off the plane in a fog of weariness and stepped into the blazing light, I saw a vision: battlefields, jungles, charred and contorted bodies of women and children. There were soldiers in the vision—young men—crawling through the mud, dodging bullets, recoiling from the explosions and the flying pieces of shrapnel. Some of the men lay lifeless in pools of their own blood. I saw a soldier lying on the ground, covering his face with his hands. "Doc, help me! Help me!" And then I saw myself, running through the crazy macabre scene with bandages and morphine, trying to bring the dead back to life.

This is why I was here—to treat the wounded. I had come to Vietnam to patch them up, keep them alive, and get them home. Others could inflict the wounds. I was committed to healing them.

I walked across the tarmac and heard someone screaming, "Soldier, get back in line!" Looking up, I saw it was the sergeant. He was talking to me.

"Get back in line, soldier, and keep it moving."

"I'm not a soldier," I said, "I'm a navy corpsman, I'm the medic."

He dismissed me with a nod of his head. "Okay, *Medic,* keep it moving."

We walked single file toward a waiting bus. A line of soldiers passed by us going in the opposite direction. They were heading to the airplane—the same airplane—we'd just left. It was their turn to go home. Maybe a year from now, I'll get to be in their place.

I looked around at the guys ahead of me. How many of them would make it? Would I make it?

Our destiny was handed to us in a boarding number when we arrived at the III Marine Air Facility (MAF) Terminal. This airport was the second busiest in the world. Cargo planes were arriving at breakneck speed from Japan, Thailand, or the Philippines delivering food and clothing, and of course, ammunition. Others transported guys going on R&R or *home.*

Jets were continuously screaming off the runways, delivering their deadly cargo wherever it was needed, maybe north of the demilitarized zone. Of course, this was only a namesake because there was plenty of action within the DMZ itself. If these planes weren't headed north, they were probably going to bail out some unit who had *hit the shit* somewhere. I hoped that wasn't the unit I was headed for. Dong Ha would be my destination.

Bob, a fellow corpsman, and I sat down and waited for our departure flight. It was hard to believe that only three days ago we were in New York, and now we were half a world away, possibly to never return. I was scared, and my mind began to race. "What would I do with the incoming? What would I do in the bush? How would things turn out?"

I was so young, just twenty years old, but one of the older men in my unit. We were all just kids.

A C-130 had just arrived, and everybody had gotten up to watch the cargo being unloaded. My curiosity got the best of me, and I wished it hadn't. I saw my first body in a bag being carried away to a cracker box (crash ambulance), and I prayed, "God, have mercy on these guys." The count began, one, two, three . . . soon it was twenty-five.

Twenty-five brave men had served their nation, and they were dead. Were these lives wasted? I thought so and cursed this godforsaken nation whose leaders wanted us to protect their interests and investments. We weren't there to help the people, just the wealthy leaders.

I could have cried as I watched the procession of cracker boxes filing down the runway with the remains of those soldiers. I could only imagine the sorrow of those twenty-five families, wives, fiancées, and girlfriends.

Once again, I prayed, "Dear God, *please* be with me."

Our flight to Dong Ha was announced, and we made our way to the gate. I had never flown in a C-130 before and was unaccustomed to being thrown around in flight, especially among our cargo of ammunition. It was announced that the airstrip in Dong Ha had been getting hit with incoming, so as soon as we landed we were to evacuate the runway as soon as possible. I sat there, chewing my fingernails, imagining every possible scenario until we landed. I think I dove out of the plane, ready to dodge any incoming.

The terminal was very small and in a rural area. Here I saw my first prisoners of war. There were two VC (Viet Cong) prisoners with cloth sacks over their heads, hands tied behind their backs, and squatting in their customary manner. There were two guards and a dog watching over them. I flashed back to the twenty-five soldiers in body bags, martyrs in my mind, and I was overcome with anger. I felt like kicking those prisoners over and over again. After all, I knew why I was here, didn't I? I was here to free the people from the communists, and they were the enemy, weren't they?

It was getting late in the day, and they sent us to the Dong Ha transit right across the road from the airstrip. Later, we were checked in and given a cot and assigned a tent. Someone eagerly asked if this area had been getting shelled, and the matter-of-fact reply was, "Not too often, but once in a while a short round will land close by." I immediately moved my cot to the tent opening, which gave me quick access to a trench, my shelter. Another first that night was the C-rations. To help wash it down, I bought myself a warm beer from some old sergeant who had been hoarding them.

This was the first day of my tour, and already I had seen and experienced so many things I would never forget. Once again, I thought about those dead soldiers' families receiving the dreaded telegram announcing their sons' deaths. Fearfully, I asked God, "What if my mother ever got one? What would she do?"

I was jolted away from my thoughts when a huge explosion boomed just behind us. Bob and I were out of the tent in a flash, much to the amusement of the other boarders of tent #3.

"No sweat," they told us. "That's outgoing. You don't hear the one that hits you."

Reluctantly, I reentered my berthing area, only to stay awake all night imagining what the events of the year could bring.

As morning came, Bob and I were assigned to Quang Tri, about five miles south of our position where division offices were housed. We were to find the division surgeon or the "division doc" as we would later call him. To our surprise, we were sent out with only directions. There were no weapons, no driver, no guide supplied, just directions. We wondered, "What the hell kind of war is this?" and then hopped on a six-by-six truck after making sure they were going to Quang Tri. We found out later they were heading to Quang Tri, just not right away. There would first be a trip to the docks to pick up a buddy who was buying some booze and marijuana from the natives in Dong Ha.

Another first opportunity arose to see the Vietnamese people. I could only think what a wretched bunch they were. They lived in shacks, which made our ghettos look like Scarsdale. There was filth, disease, and lots of children. I could only believe this was a godforsaken nation. I saw kids standing on the roadside begging and smoking, some giving us the finger. It caused me to feel bitter, void of sorrow or compassion.

"Is this what America is fighting to save? Is this what those twenty-five guys died for?" I asked myself. My anger swelled as I dodged rocks those little bastards were throwing at us because we hadn't given them anything.

After picking up the guy, we headed south to our destination along the dust-brewing road. Kids were still begging, and others were giving us the thumbs-up sign. I didn't want to notice that.

At the small base in Quang Tri, we quickly found the surgeon general's office, and after a short welcome, we were assigned to the Ninth Marines unit. Again, we were off in our not-ready-for-combat state; however, once we got there, things were to change.

Bob and I again were stationed together at the 1/9 BAS (First Battalion, Ninth Regiment, Battalion Aid Station). It would be a day or two before we reached our company because they had just left Khe Sanh and were manning lines at C-2, which was by Con Thien, the northern most outpost. In our orientation, they let us know that 1/9 was a hard luck outfit, especially Bravo Company. We were again warned of the potential enemy besides the obvious hazards, heat, snakes, rats, malaria, and even tigers. As soon as they could make up some unit ones (our bag of tricks), we would be leaving for the bush.

The next day we were issued all our jungle gear, the helmet, flak jacket, and of course our weapons. This game was for keeps. It wouldn't be long, and we would be leaving an area that offered us a hot meal and a show in the evening in trade for C-rats and air strikes.

I was given a break, however. The chief told me to stay around and go on the road sweeps in the morning. No complaints from me. I prepared myself for my new assignment and hoped it would last awhile.

6:00 a.m. came early, but I was ready. As soon as I got on the truck, the marines knew I was green with my nice new fatigues. They were green ones too and offered some helpful tips that would be to my benefit in the future. Once the truck started rolling, fear overwhelmed me. I became so uncertain of myself and wondered if I would freeze when someone needed me.

At the gate, we were greeted by a tank and two quad-fifties which is a truck with four fifty-caliber machine guns mounted on it. A sense of security was beginning to settle my fear. Our area to sweep was from Dong Ha to Cam Lo, a refugee village a few miles to the north. After we arrived at our checkpoint, we disembarked the vehicles, and I fell in behind some soul brother who told me to stick close to him. He promised to watch over me that day. When we got up the road a ways with the engineers, our lead element found a small mine and quickly disengaged it, and again further up we stopped again to disengage another mine waiting for some unsuspecting vehicle to trip it.

While we were stopped, a young child of about ten came up to me from out of the rice paddy with his water buffalo. He came up to me saying, "Bac Si," and pointed to a cut on his finger. The brother looking out for me told him to beat it. I joined in, waving my weapon at him. I wanted to help him with his cut, but I remembered what they had told us in field medical service school. Never trust anyone, young or old. The docs had to be especially careful. A kid could come up to corpsmen and show them a wound. When they were being bandaged, he would be automatically pointed out to a sniper hiding in the bush. It had happened before and could happen to me.

As the sweep continued, we came across more children on the roadside, and I made certain they stayed away by waving my weapon. We remounted our trucks and headed back to Dong Ha by way of Cam Lo. Going through Cam Lo, I could see who was really being hurt by the war. I began to see the suffering firsthand.

The kids were lined up on both sides of the road as if they were watching a parade go by, only they were hoping to scavenge some food the marines might throw off the trucks. Their bellies were distended from malnutrition, some had limbs missing, and others were undoubtedly wandering around without their parents or a home. As we passed, the children began waving and giving us the thumbs-up. I felt bad for not giving that boy a Band-Aid for his finger. I wished I had something useful to throw to these children.

At that moment, I was changed. I sensed the appreciation from the people, the children. I knew they needed our help. It was then I looked back on the day I cursed this nation and all the people in it and regretted it. Because of the negative actions of a few on the road to Quang Tri, I generalized in my mind all of the people to be a wretched bunch.

"Perhaps they will be here tomorrow, and I can throw them some candy or C-rats," I decided.

When we got back from our sweep that day, I got my new mailing address and wrote my folks and my girlfriend, Lynne, and told them I was glad to be here no matter what the outcome. I was glad I could do my part and hoped I would do it well. Our country was willing to sacrifice so much to keep the reigns on communism, and I was now part of their mission.

On the next day's sweep, we came across a case of mortars almost immediately. When we came to the point where we disembarked from the trucks the day before, I began to look for the little fellow I had neglected to treat. As we proceeded down the road, I gave up hopes of finding him when suddenly there he was, standing in a rice paddy with his buffalo. I motioned for him to come over to me, but he just backed away until I baited him with some gum I bought at the PX. After giving him the gum, I cleaned his wound and dressed it for him. I was astonished when he smiled and in clear English said, "Thank you, Boss C." As he walked away smiling, I had a warm feeling inside.

When we reached Dong Ha, I was greeted by corpsmen that had gone to field medical school service school with me, Drs. Stever, Young, and Provience. I only ran across a few of my former classmates during my tour of Vietnam. Seeing these corpsmen come in meant that I would be leaving in the morning. I was going to be a marine, something I had never anticipated or wanted.

Waking early, I prepared to take on my new job. This was going to be an extreme change from working in a hospital where I took orders. Now I was on my own. I would be solely responsible for the physical and mental well-being of the men within my unit. This included everything from giving malaria tabs to performing emergency treatments such as tracheotomies or CPR in order to save a life. Bob and I stopped at C-3 to meet our battalion surgeon, and then we're on our way to C-2 to meet the guys who would place their lives in my hands and mine in theirs. I just prayed I would *never* fail them.

When I checked into the aid station at C-2, I was greeted by Doc Stead whose place I would be taking. This had been his ninth month in the bush, and most corpsmen got out after six. Rest assured he was glad to see me. I would soon be humping the hills of Vietnam with the grunts and in some ways would be looking forward to it. I soon found out that Doc Stead was well respected and promised myself that I too would earn their respect. While at C-2, the guys managed to pool their money and buy a case or two of beer a week. By the time I came out of one hutch, a guy named Zack from Shy Town had given me beer already. He said, "Doc, don't forget us, and we won't forget you." I didn't fully understand what he meant, but in time it became very clear.

As I went down to the first squad's hutch, I saw they were getting ready to go out on an ambush. Doc Stead said he would go out since it would be his last. He was leaving for the rear in the morning, and before he left he introduced me to the men who would eventually become very important in my life.

First came DJ Lynch from Queens, New York. He hadn't been home in almost two years and could hardly wait for the next two months to pass, for then he was homeward bound. DJ could have been the poster boy for the marines with the caption, "This is how we build men!" stamped on his forehead. Around the squad, he pulled a lot of weight and was very respected.

Another New Yorker, Paul Flagg from Jamestown, was a big, bulky guy, built like a battleship. He loved to write letters home. This guy became our machine gunner, a job he was well built for.

Steve Woffe from Illinois was our 3.5 man. This weapon was like a bazooka and very cumbersome. The terrain and tropic vegetation didn't contribute any to help manage it more easily. He swore at that thing like a drill sergeant at a new recruit in boot camp. Steve was the most generous and thoughtful guys I was to meet. Besides looking out for other guys in the field, he also made his care packages from home community property. One of the best treats was when we got to share a canned ham in the jungles of Vietnam for Easter. I took the webbing out of the inside of my helmet and put the ham in it. We heated it up over the fire. Civilized food from home, what a holiday meal!

Our nation's capitol yielded our next squad member, Jerry Wright. All he talked about was his wife and son, and he carried their pictures in his helmet at all times. His family was anxiously awaiting his return back to Washington, DC, all the while trying to get him home on a hardship transfer. His wife had suffered two nervous breakdowns since the beginning of his tour. I always wished it would hurriedly go through because Jerry was our point man and looked death in the eye with every step he took. His son deserved having a father, especially the good one that Jerry was. Jerry never got the transfer but had an angel walking beside him until his safe return five months later.

There were others like Barney from Houston, Texas, and a big mouth named Buff from North Carolina who was quite undependable. His worst offense was falling asleep on watch, endangering the lives of the squad, and that was unforgivable. After two months, he was transferred to a CAP (Civic Action Program), and we were glad to see him go.

Philip Outlaw from Miami was Jerry's back up for point man. During his tour, he earned a Bronze Star for Valor for saving a buddy's life.

Georgia was the home of Cecil Saliburry, better known as Junior, a very capable machine gunner. Junior kept the spirits of the squad lifted by telling us about his numerous drinking and speeding experiences back home. His philosophy was that when your time came, that was it. It was out of your control. Junior didn't have much respect for the natives but would do anything for the squad. He always shared his booze and was a good man to have around when you *hit the shit.*

Walter Chicca was in 'Nam from Philadelphia and not even a United States citizen. Even so, he was willing to do his part for a nation that had accepted his family. He came from somewhere close to the Soviet Union and got really pissed off when he was called "The Russian."

Walt was one of my guinea pigs. He had jungle rot, and I had to experiment to get the right combination of medication to heal it. Walt was wounded with me on June 18 and would go home because of his injuries.

From Arkansas came Billy Bradley. He was African-American and one of the best men I would meet in Vietnam. Billy wanted to be a doctor and was very eager to learn any little hints I had. He used to freely discuss the *niggers* and the *Negroes* who were hindering and helping the black Americans. Billy was one of the few black guys I knew who stayed in the bush his whole tour. He frowned upon the brother who remained in the rear with their tape recorders listening to their soul music while we were out in the bush doing our job and theirs. One time in particular, we were leaving on an operation, and one of the brothers gave Bill the Black Power symbol. His reply was the finger, which showed he wanted nothing to do with the *niggers* who weren't as *bad* as they thought they were in their old neighborhood. Billy was wounded on August 22, 1968, while covering me with his own body.

Dave, our squad leader from Louisiana, left two months later and was replaced by Jim Simons of Lansing, Michigan. Jim, a good friend, was plagued with jungle rot from the start and became another guinea pig. Simons eventually went to the rear because of his spreading jungle rot and was replaced with Henry Cannon, a Tennessee ridge runner. He couldn't get along with anyone and always hoped to see some action just like a little "lifer." Everyone enjoyed the day; one of the guys decked him and put him in his place.

Our radioman was Terry Landa from Detroit, Michigan, the only grunt I knew who did a complete thirteen months out in the bush and *never* wounded. The only time he left the bush was for R&R. He had seen the rigors of war but of another kind, the riots of 1965. Terry was frequently called "the nose" and was one of the most respected guys in the platoon, and if someone needed help, he would be right there.

I would meet many others, but these were the men whom I would so closely come to know during my tour. I became their doctor, confessor, father, best friend, and guidance counselor. They looked to me when they needed someone to talk to or patch them up. This was my time. I was ready to accept the challenge.

May 8, at dusk

As the sun began setting in the distance, giving way to the peace and serenity of the evening, my squad prepared themselves for another night ambush. I asked around to make sure I had everything, and before long we were on our way. This would be my first ambush and night out in the real bush. We began filing out the north gate as soon as the shadow of night fell upon us. Down the road about a half mile and then in a quarter mile, we formed an L-shaped ambush to catch any infiltrating enemy by surprise. The night went slowly without incident, except for one not so bright move on my part. We were standing lines at C-2 when I decided I needed a smoke, which I rarely did. Without thinking, I just lit up. Jim dove at me, smothering the light and chided, "Are you trying to get us all shot?" On a clear night, you could see a lit cigarette two miles away and a lit match five miles. Luckily, I adapted quickly.

As the dawn crept in, we packed up and humped it home. Some of the guys went to sleep, and others went to man the lines. I talked with the guys for a while, but before long I was asleep on my rubber mattress, commonly referred to as the "rubber bitch."

I had just gotten to sleep when another corpsman, introducing himself as Doc Hamman, woke me up. We were divided among three squads, my permanent one being the first, the third, and the second was our toss up, which was going out on patrol. We flipped a coin, and my "heads" call lost the toss. By 12:30 p.m. I was ready and in front of the second squad's hutch for a one o'clock departure. Last night was my first ambush, and today was my first patrol.

We traveled down the road in a staggered column, and I was somewhere in the middle. Upon reaching checkpoint #1, we moved off to the side of the road and took five. It was here I met David Wright with whom I was to become great friends. In time, I would come to call him "Angel," after his girl whom he constantly talked about. He was going to marry her when he got home.

I met another guy who seemed like he had been out there for quite a while, and he passed on helpful information about getting along easier out in the bush. I remember one simple, yet significant piece of advice on how to keep my helmet cooler. It was really common sense, but I had overlooked it. He said I should turn my helmet right side up while not wearing it to deflect some of the heat. Leaving it upside down would leave the webbing exposed to absorb more heat. This always stuck with me because it taught me to *think* at all times.

When our break ended, the squad leader decided we were on the wrong side of the road, so we hiked over to the other side and searched our perimeter. We were looking for signs of recent travel on certain trails and any other irregularities. This reminded me more of a Boy Scout outing rather than an intelligence gathering. They always said the difference between the Marine Corps and the Boy Scouts is that the Boy Scouts had adult advisors. From what I had experienced so far, I began to believe there was some validity to that statement.

After following through our previously plotted patrol route, we took another five. The sun was beating down as we relaxed on a little knoll not far from the perimeter. Suddenly, out of nowhere we were taking fire. An order to pull back was passed. I flung myself face down and could see the ground spitting up dirt all around me. We radioed back to our command to see if the line could see anything. Waiting for our reply and further orders, we regrouped only to find one guy missing. We reported our MIA, and two of us decided to go back to where we had taken fire since he had probably been hit. It came over the radio that he had run to the perimeter and that our guys on the frontline were the ones firing at us. I realized that we not only had to watch out for the enemy but the GI's as well. It was still better to know that it was friendly fire instead of *Charlie* since we were going out on another ambush tonight.

That night we left at the same time, went to the same area, and came back at dawn. This went on for three consecutive days, and even I knew this wasn't an elusive military tactic. On the fourth straight ambush, another platoon was sent in. They were caught in a crossfire no more than 100 feet from the gate, and luckily there were no casualties. At times I wondered if we were just bait to attract the enemy, or if this was really the military tactics of our well-disciplined higher echelon.

May 12, Mother's Day

The first thing I did that day was to wish all mothers a safe and speedy return of their sons, especially mine. Then I fell into my routine of checking my squad for foot trouble and jungle rot because we were heading out the next morning for a three-day sweep. Malaria and salt tablets were passed out and rationed. I stepped out of the bunker to check the guys from the second squad and was nearly wiped out by a mule, a Jeep minus the chassis. It was delivering our water ration when the break line failed. Fortunately, I managed to escape injury by jumping on the roof of our bunker. Nonetheless, I was adapting quite well to my new environment and began taking pride in having my men physically ready at all times.

The last few days, besides going on patrols and ambushes, were spent fixing our shitter and figuring out how to build a shower. Material was scarce, but I managed to confiscate some things. Besides being their medicine man, I was also the sanitation engineer and was responsible for the elimination of waste and keeping the area as clean as possible. Rats continued to be a problem, and at times it was wise to leave some food out for them, sort of like an offering. A rat bite could be nasty and possibly result in a case of rabies. Guys from other platoons managed to evade certain operations by claiming a rat bite, but that was quite a painful way of getting out of the bush for fourteen days. Those shots in the abdomen must have been hell. In all my time, I had only one case to treat, and it was for real.

That afternoon about 4:30 p.m. we boarded trucks that would take us to Cam Lo, a refugee village just outside of Camp Evans. Just one year ago, these people were driven from their fields and homes and forced to live in Cam Lo which is 20 miles from Trung Luong, their ancestral grounds. Operation Beau Charger was to soon be under way, and the soil these people tilled would soon become a battlefield. Without warning, they were herded onto trucks after ID's were checked. Those without ID's were retained. Trucks were supplied by the Marine Corps but driven by South Vietnamese soldiers to maintain the fix that this was a Government of South Vietnam venture.

These people had a different culture and believed they shouldn't die in a strange place away from their ancestors. That link to their heritage was how they could achieve their Buddhist version of heaven. That fear and the fact they had lost their land was sufficient enough to demolish these people and turn them against us. Without a shot being fired, the U.S. and the GVN (Government of South Vietnam) had managed to destroy all the hopes and emotional stability of the thirteen thousand people involved. Acts such as these did not help our winning the "other war," which was pacification. Without this, Vietnam would never experience true peace. Our higher echelon or professional soldiers for the most part had engrossed themselves in a military victory and had bypassed the obvious. Give a child candy, and the next time he sees, you he'll be friendly. Slap him, and you have made an enemy. We destroyed these people's homes and lives. They would forever be suspicious and outright with us.

As we began to dig in, I could see what we had done to destroy these people. Young boys were selling their sisters barely into their teens. "Sucky, sucky, fucky, fucky" became common call for sex while around a village. The black market supplied the people with booze and soda and just about any other consumer product you could possibly need. A Coke could cost you $1, and a bottle of booze, which at the PX sold for about $3, was sold by the natives for at least $10. You had to watch what you bought because it damn well might have crushed glass in it. The word was passed to not buy any of the native's products, especially the marijuana. After they left, we continued to dig in.

Before dusk, we all sat around eating our C-rats, giving what was left to some of the children who were still milling around. Everyone was talking about women at home, and I imagined Lynne and I sitting on a beach blanket together, sipping wine. Everything faded away when darkness blanketed the evening and the watches began.

At 2:00 a.m. we were all packed and ready to leave. We walked until 5:30 a.m. and then dug in again. That day, we swept the valley. As we began to return to our dug-in positions, we encountered sniper fire. Rest assured that night I was wide awake.

The night went quickly, and there were no incidents. Before we knew it, we were off to take another objective. We had to cross the river which was relief from the heat. Many of us fell in just to cool off, but when we reached the other side, there was action in store for us. Upon reaching the far bank, the enemies opened up with small arms and mortars. They must have been on the run because they missed us by a long shot. Air strikes were called, and we dug in. Tanks were called in, and before long it looked like a combat movie being filmed with the marines on the assault, except this was for real. We laboriously made our way up one hill, and then we're told to return. Once we got back, the mortars began to fall again as another platoon got into a firefight.

By this time, we were back at the riverbank. The air show continued with the brilliant tongues of fire from the napalm, licking the valley as the NVA attempted to retreat. As we were sitting back, letting the heavy equipment do the work, the enemy managed to get one more barrage of mortars to hit our position. After the first impact, everyone was down, but clearly the calls for "Corpsman" rang out. Almost immediately I began running toward the call. This would be my first chance to treat a casualty, and I had to do my best. Some of the guys yelled, "Doc, get down!" I couldn't stop myself and continued to run, even though mortars were still falling around us. I guess I ran more out of fear than anything else.

When I reached the first guy who was screaming in hysteria, it was the guy who gave me the tip about keeping my helmet cool. He caught a piece of shrapnel in the eye. All I could do was put a dressing over it and keep it immobilized. Sgt. Jay managed to catch a piece of shrapnel in his butt. They always said he was getting his ass in trouble anyway. Another fellow messed up his shoulder and caught shrapnel in his kidney region. Before we knew it, a chopper was on its way to pick up our wounded. Once more we attempted to take the hill but were driven back. We had to do something quickly because it was going to rain, and it would be hell trying to make it back across the river with the enemy after us.

Steady rain began, and in just a half an hour, we got about two or three inches of precipitation. The word was passed to get back across the river to the positions we held the preceding night. Water that was waist high on the first trip across was now chest deep with one hell of a current. Weapons were held high over our heads in order to prevent them from getting any wetter. Six guys lost their weapons as the swift current managed to pull them off their balance. It was either let your weapon go, or go with it. One guy lost everything but his clothing and cartridge belt.

Once we reached the other side, we took up our previous positions which were now flooded. I remember asking for the first watch because I figured someone would keep me company. It was still raining and the guys were wondering why I was standing watch. After all, I didn't have to. Corpsmen were not subject to standing watch as stated by the Geneva Convention, but I felt it was my tail too, so I should do my part. I wanted to cut my buddies a break. If I had not stood watch, it would have meant more time they would be awake. We were all in the same boat, so why should I get any special treatment?

As my watch began, the rain began to let up slightly, and the drops that were still dripping from the trees put my nerves on edge. I stayed motionless for my hour-and-a-half. All went well, except for the fact I was really cold. When my watch was over, I curled in between two guys, so their body heat would keep me warm. I felt more secure knowing there was someone on each side of me. If someone had snuck up on me, I would be screwed. I didn't know a thing about M-16s. I moved closer to one of the guys in my hole. At one time, a firefly flew toward me, and I thought it was someone with a cigarette. I froze and then realized what it was. It came time for my second watch which seemed to take forever, and then it was morning. We crossed the river again, this time on tanks and swept the valley. The VC had vanished during the night. We walked for almost eight hours through rice paddy after rice paddy in the blazing sun. This was really a chore, but we met no opposition.

We finally reached the road that connected C-2 and C-3. Six-bys picked us up and drove us back to C-2. What a relief. Clean clothes and a hot meal were in store for us.

May 16

Back at C-2, but not for long. The following day, we were headed to the Washout a little south of there. During the day, we rested, and a few guys were smoking grass that Cunningham had gotten. He had a little arrangement with a girl he met on R&R who kept him supplied. We passed around the pipe. It was one of the ways to escape the reality of war, something everyone had to do in one way or another. We were standing lines with barbed wire fences and a minefield in front of us with nothing to worry about. In the distance, we could see the air show, yet to us at present it seemed somewhat of a fireworks display. Smoking grass became a means of relaxing but only to the guys in a rather secure area. I never saw anyone smoking in the bush, but in the rear, it was common practice even for some of the officers.

As the day went by, we were informed of our mission in the morning. 6:30 a.m. and we were on our way. The six-bys were loaded, and we were off to the Washout to stand lines. Here we would get two hot meals a day and a place to bathe. The food beat the C-rats, and the creek was a means of evading the ever-present heat. As soon as we were settled in, we made our way to the stream. I sat in the middle of the stream with a rack for a backrest, just enjoying the hell out of the water flowing over my crusty body. We made it a must to go there three times a day. It was anticipated that we would stay there awhile, but soon we were headed back to C-2. Two hours after we left, the Washout took incoming which caused considerable damage and ended the life of the chaplain's assistant. C-2 got a few rounds also, and from then on, we stood in the trenches while waiting in the chow line.

As the days passed, we managed to get enough material to build our shower. The ammo boxes were filled with dirt and stacked up. A 55-gallon drum was stolen and vigorously scrubbed to become our water container. A piece of rubber tubing managed to spray the water out when pushed. Everyone was anxious to try our new shower; however, we didn't have any water. I was the first to try it after water arrived, but mail call came around, and the showers were quickly forgotten.

There it was, my first letter. One was from my mother and the other from Lynne, a seventeen pager. I couldn't have imagined it as I fought back the tears. After reading a few hundred times, I put it in my helmet, always to keep it with me. Anytime I got depressed, I would reread it and feel reassured there would be someone waiting for me when I got home.

That night, they had air strikes in the vicinity of Cua Viet. Everyone was out to watch it as we had every night before. The guys who had been there for some time expand especially at Khe Sanh. Our sister company, Alpha, had lost twenty-some guys in one night because some guys had fallen asleep on watch. This is why all of us got pissed off at Buff so often when he fell asleep on his watches. In one day at Khe Sanh, they had taken over one thousand two hundred rounds of and mortars. There was also the day when a jet got shot out of the sky, and the pilot flew over the base and ejected, landing safely within the perimeter, and the resupplies by air drops were always brought up when we had the chance to sit around and talk in a group. I had no stories to tell, and I hoped that it would stay that way, but I knew different. My day would come.

Another thing that came up when the guys were reminiscing was the night Sack and another guy were in the suicide hole. This was a bunker which was the point furthest out from the base, which was a listening post. They had fallen asleep on watch, and two enemies, supplied only with hand grenades and knives, made their way through the barbed wire and mine field and tripped forward, heading for our CP (Command Post). They almost made it, but were turned back and killed in the trench lines. Would I ever experience anything like these episodes? I hoped not, but time would discard my wish.

As morning came around, we got the water for the shower, and I eagerly made my way into it. As I was in there, they passed the word to pack up. We were pulling out, just our luck. We just get it finished, and we pull out. Little did we know that we would never return to C-2. We were ready to leave by one o'clock, but as four o'clock came around, we were still there. As we were waiting, they told us that we were going to land in a hot zone, so be ready for anything. With this, Doc Hannan went to load his .45, and it accidentally discharged, striking his hand. I would now have to take care of the whole damn platoon by myself, now something I would get accustomed to. We landed at Camp Little Big John at Cua Viet. Before I was leaving Vietnam, they would have an R&R center at Cua Viet where USO shows would someday be observed by troops who the day before were humping through the bush.

The next day, we pulled out to sweep the area. We traveled for a few hours when we came under heavy sniper fire. This was only to stall us from reaching the main force that was retreating. The operation became known as 0024 Napoleon-Saline, and it was here that I would see my first dead enemy, and we would capture some prisoners of war. The snipers finally ceased, and we moved on; however, as we moved on, we again encountered sniper fire.

My squad was sent out to silence them. At this time, I was kind of gunshy [sic] and followed them out. I used to carry six frags and looked like a hard-core grunt rather than a corpsman. Sitting behind the hedgerow, I heard a bullet whiz past my head. The snipers had managed to keep our whole company down, especially me, after that, so a Bird dog was called in to help us find their positions. The Bird dog is a spotter plane which would soon make way for the bigger and better Bronco. Arty followed and came pretty damn close to our positions. By this time, he was silenced, and we continued on our way as dusk began to settle. We were to link up with another outfit, but someone screwed up and took the wrong way, which became common with the infamous captain among our ranks.

After stumbling around in the dark for four hours, we linked up; however, behind our position were three dead gooks whose bodies were decaying, and the stench was nauseating. When morning came around, we began checking their persons and collecting their belts and other souvenirs. I managed to get one of their canteens, an ID card, and some North Vietnamese stamps. This was just the start of a treasure hunt that would reveal North Vietnamese money, Russian-made watches, and medicine. Medicine that said it was donated by the people of Berkley. Just how true this is, I do not know, but it made you think just how many people back home were on your side.

We soon moved after burying the remains of the enemy soldiers. As human beings, you had to feel sorry for the NVA and respect them for dying bravely in their civil war, a civil war taken over by the Americans. Why should we get involved as we did? After all, how many of the Vietnamese fought in our civil war? It was an internal problem being fought by those involved with the outsider only being spectators and advisors. Why couldn't we play that role and give them a little pride in themselves to do a job they must do for themselves and not done for them. 0025

Anyway, we kept moving, sweeping the area. At one point, we sat in by a river. I checked it out to see if the water was potable, but while crossing it, I stepped on a body that had rocks tied to him to keep him under the water. They told us in FMS that the gooks did this to spoil the drinking H2O, but I didn't believe it. I passed the word not to drink it and had a patrol go across the river to a well where the ARVN were getting their water. Little fish were still swimming in it, so it must be drinkable. We were doing their fighting, so they gladly helped us fill the canteens we had carried with us. Small groups of men began searching the area and came back with fifty-caliber machine guns, numerous small arms, a mortar tube, frags, and other gear left by the fleeing enemy. After they brought back their find, we had to search the area again and stockpile all the ammo and the rest of the weapons we found. We would then blow it up.

As we were searching, we came across numerous bodies. Some guys were getting what marijuana they could from the dead soldiers. It was common knowledge that most gooks carried around a pouch of grass, or a pipe smoker would have tobacco. Others who were nervier went into their pockets and got their wallets along with a handful of maggots. Some took those stench-smelling belts from the decomposing bodies and wore them while one guy in particular grooved on the gold teeth of the dead. He kicked one out of a guy whose head was completely severed. I asked him what the fuck his bag was, and he moved on. He was definitely one of those casualties of war; not physical, but mental. It's a shame that people are as cruel as in war. Could you imagine the horror of finding just a foot in a shoe or just a backbone of a human being who had met such a savage death from our bombs? What a shame for the world that we have put our ingenuity into work such as this.

As I moved on, I found a radio bunker with two bodies in it and informed our squad leader who had someone go in and get all the radio gear out that also would be blown away.

All the ammo was piled in one area with the rest of the gear, and the engineers were setting a delayed fuse to blow it while we moved back to our positions. As we began moving away, the 0026 ARVN's moved in to see what they could find. However, before they reached it, it went off, and they hightailed it back to their area. All night they prep fired on the area and at one time dropped a couple 1,000-pound bombs which shook the earth like a quake. As we moved in, we found no opposition, but the next day we would capture our first POW.

As night came around, we were positioned in the river with one fire team on the other side. The enemy was trapped and would try anything to get out, so we were to be on a constant alert. Our hole was right on the riverbank with a paddy dike to our right. When it got dark, it was impossible to see anything on the other side of the dike, so I put some of the casing from a napalm canister next to it, and if a gook tried to get by, we would have to hear him. When morning came around after a peaceful night on our front, we were informed that two marines from another outfit had their throats slashed because someone fell asleep on watch. I guess they will never learn. The enemy once again had eluded us.

We started about 9:00 a.m. and went through a deserted village. Hand grenades were thrown into all bunkers and huts. I was getting my rocks off throwing frags into the bunkers, and at one point when our sergeant told someone to blow that hutch I said "No sweat, sergeant. I got it." Sure I thought that I was the John Wayne of the Marine Corps. I'm glad I did not keep that act up too long. Upon entering the third village, we captured our first prisoners. I remember carrying one of the wounded gooks away while an AP photographer was getting it down on film. I treated him the best I could and took his belt as a souvenir. Before leaving, we had accumulated 18 POW. The tanks were with us now, and we traded the weapons we found for beer and soda that they had with them. The two rifles I had found netted a half case of soda which was deeply appreciated by the guys in my squad.

As we came across a rice paddy leading to the fourth village which had marines behind it, we encountered a small sized enemy force, which were trapped between us. As we advanced forward, we came under heavy automatic weapon fire. This was their stand, somewhat similar to Custer's. Woffe got his first chance to fire 0027 his .35 at a small grave monument which was sheltering a sniper. He just missed it, but the tankers didn't. As we advanced, Taber from Chicago was with me. Quite a character. He had collected over $500 in NVA money, plus a Russian watch and was longing to get home. Once he got home, he was going to marry a pen pal who he had never seen. I asked if he was going to be married for only a year, his reply was "Why so long?"

Anyway, as we were advancing, they hollered for Taber to get a certain position with his M-79. This is a grenade launcher. However, the first round wouldn't fire, nor the second or third, so there we were with only two .45s in the face of the enemy. We continued to advance, however, and as we caught up to Flagg with the machine gun, I spotted a sniper hole. Someone threw in a grenade while hollering "Fire in the hole." If there was anyone in there, he wasn't around anymore. It proved to be empty however. It was one of the positions that they were firing at us from because fresh blood was found in it and we captured three wounded NVA, one of which undoubtedly was hit in there. Besides the three wounded, we also captured five others. The rest were killed. After we reached the marines on the other side of the village, we turned around and headed back sweeping the area. All the equipment was loaded on the tanks and the long walk back to our previous positions was under way. One tank became disabled, and Woffe and Buff were told to remain with it wherever it went.

The rains had begun, and no relief was in sight. Once we got back to our position, we were going to be choppered out. That's the only thing we had to look forward to. After sweeping the area, we finally got back to our previously held positions. Going through one area, we had to be extremely careful. Scattered about were round objects about the size of a tennis ball. Inside it held BBs which were suppose to go off once they hit the ground. They were dispersed over the area by an airplane; however, they never went off. Perhaps they would if we disturbed them. So like a porcupine making love, we proceeded very carefully.

As we were waiting for the choppers, they had a check of all the personnel. They couldn't find Buff and Woffe when everyone knew they were with the tanks. Instead of calling the tank headquarters to see if they had arrived with them, they made us hump back with all our gear to the spot where we left them. Everyone was exhausted already, and I really doubted if I could make it there and back again. We had been walking since nine in the morning, and it was now somewhere around 4:00. The rain was a relief from the sweltering heat, but after a while it made traveling impossible.

While advancing, everyone was yelling for our two lost soldiers who were probably back in Dong Ha by now. We began to curse those fools. We knew damn well that they would be back with the tankers, but you try to explain something logical to a lifer, and you'll soon see how fruitless it is. Perhaps if we had a career man as our commander, we could talk some sense; however, we didn't. Our commander was looking for a name for himself as well as a promotion and decoration. The more the better.

Reaching the furthest point, we had reached before, we turned around and headed back again toward the landing zone. While on the way back, everyone sang the Marine Corps hymn, "Him, him, fuck him." By this time, we were slipping and sliding through the mud which was about a foot in spots. Walking became a burden, but we trudged on knowing once we reached the LZ, we would be heading in after about five days in the bush. Hot food, a shower, clean clothes, and a beer were the driving force which helped us to continue. Also we couldn't wait until we got our hands on Woffe and Buff, even though it wasn't their fault.

We soon were touching down at Dong Ha where our rear was. It was good to be back where mail, packages, and a few comforts were at our disposal. And when we saw our two MIA, we forgot about that burdensome walk looking for them. We were actually glad to see them again and forgot about the whole matter as they helped us with our gear.

My mail consisted of a variety of letters, all of which I enjoyed tremendously. First, I read the ones from my folks. Everything was fine on the home front, and all their prayers were for my swift and safe return. The next one came from Joe McCormick, my longtime and best friend back home. He had married Sue, and everything was going just great. Perhaps once I got home, I too would be joining the ranks of the married. I could hardly wait.

The next letter came from a darling of a girl whom I had met while attending corps school. She has written ever since, and in the future would continue to do so. Once I get home, I will have to meet Jenni again, even if it means going all the way to Zumbrota, Minnesota. These are the ones

I've been waiting for, however, those from Lynne. Almost. Almost one day telling me how much she misses me and can hardly wait until I get home. Believe me, I couldn't either. You know it's true that absence makes the heart grow fonder if there was really love in the first place. A love that could endure all the hardships that life has in store for them can make this challenge a testimony of their undying love. It goes both ways over here, but is the perfect test for the right partner.

While I have the time, I think I'll write as many letters as I can. Seeing everything is fine at home, I think I'll just let them know that everything is as well as can be expected here.

Tonight we would be having a cookout with hamburgers and hot dogs, also cold beer and soda. Besides everything else, we would be sleeping in cots tonight, a far cry from our accustomed handpicked area on the ground. While the party was going on, I went to our BAS to get a few supplies, and who do I meet by Sibe, a fellow corpsman who had been stationed with me in Jacksonville, Florida. We reminisced about old times over a few beers which made us feel as though we were home again.

May 31, 1968.

I woke up to a beautiful morning, even though it was in Vietnam. Anyway, it had to be a nice day because it was Paula's birthday. Believe it or not, I still loved her, but not like Lynne. Going with a girl for better than three years will always keep those good times fresh in your mind. I guess you just can't forget about your first real love anyway. She got married a month before I came to Vietnam, which made things hard to accept, seeing I never knew she was engaged or going steady. Those letters I had received were really deceiving, but that was all over now, and I truly hope she is happy. As they say, it's better to have lost in love than to have never loved at all. Thinking of this, I thanked God for the experience, for she was really a wonderful girl, and I could never forget her.

The day went by slowly with everyone relaxing. Taking in the peace and quiet of such a lovely day helped you to forget a war was going on. As the day went on, I was called to treat some fellow who had become a heat victim after lying outside in the sun all day. We got a vehicle and headed toward the BAS. A clear airway was established, clothes removed, the cool soaks begun. Upon reaching the BAS, we started an IV, and before long everything was back to normal.

Once we got back to our area, they told us to be ready to move out by six o'clock that night. We would be going out on a company-size ambush south of Dong Ha. We were carrying six meals, so we anticipated a long stay. As 6:00 came around, we were on our way out the south gate. We walked for eight hours during the night. It was dark as hell, and we were lucky that we hadn't lost anyone. About two hours out of the gate, someone tripped a booby trap which is unusual in the northern part of the Nam.

The NVA, which operated in that area, generally keep to conventional warfare; whereas the Viet Cong, who remain in the south for the most part, resorted to guerilla warfare tactics. The marines in the I-corps would rather face the NVA than the VC at least for the most part, whereas those to the south would prefer the VC. I couldn't imagine with every step I took I could face death by setting off a booby trap. Not me. I would much rather face a well-equipped, well-organized army.

Some said that it was a grenade thrown by one of our men anyway. After the explosion, the ever familiar sound of "Corpsman" rang out. A guy, who everyone called Six, got it pretty good in the arm; and Doc Quinn, a great guy and fine corpsman, had caught a piece of shrapnel in the back. As I ran down to them, I was hoping and praying that another one wouldn't go off because I would hate to get hit. After they were treated, we sent them back to Dong Ha, and we proceeded on.

As the night went on, we encountered no other hang-ups, except the terrain. At one point, we climbed down a ravine which had a nearly vertical drop. How no one was injured is beyond me, but with our human chain we proceeded. Around 2:00 a.m. we settled down on the ridge of a small valley pass. Nothing happened. But when dawn broke, we were on our way back to Dong Ha. Once we reached there, we would be leaving again. It took eight hours to get to our night position, but only two to return to the base. Once we returned, we found out we didn't have to go out after all, but our eager company commander took us out anyway. After all, how could he ever get a promotion resting in the rear?

As twelve o'clock rolled around, we loaded on six-bys which would take us to the Rock Pile. A year before, there was a fierce battle here, and it became a prime news scene. After the battle was over, they found an enemy hospital in a cave just behind the infamous Rock Pile. Gunners were even firing on the GIs. It was now June 1, and upon reaching our new home, we decided that this would definitely be a nice place to stay. After all, we had hot food, a shower, and a place to swim that was equipped with a Tarzan swing. We would go to Outpost Ben (OP Ben), which was about a mile walk from the main base. Climbing the hill became a chore, and after a while we had our rations delivered to us. Mail call came nearly every day, and the morale was high. This would be a place to relax with our only duties being a few patrols and manning an outlook.

We worked hard the first few days to get the area cleaned up and make it livable. Our "throne" (the outhouse) was rebuilt in order to keep the flies out and letting you use toilet paper rather than have the flies wipe you clean. The flies just don't learn. You swat them, but they keep coming back for more. The only thing that surpassed the number of flies was the ever present mosquitoes, which carry malaria that a good deal of our American troops serving in Nam gets. Another threat to our health was the numerous rats. They were big and didn't scare easily; however, after a few days with our rat traps and poison, we managed to bring them under relatively safe control.

The first week went by rather quickly with our only chore being to observe the area. Besides ourselves on the hill, we also had a few Army guys who manned the dusters, which are small tanks. Also we had a tank and its crew from the Marine Corps. The four guys from the tank soon became friends with my quad, and every time they went to Camp Carroll, they managed to bring a case or two of beer back for us. One fellow who was from Mamaroneck, New York, lived up the street from a corps school was a buddy of mine, Paul Bavello. Solvo was another member of the crew and came from New Jersey. He and I were to get tight in the next few weeks. When I told them I was from Poughkeepsie, New York, they asked if I knew a Terry Bochenio [sic], which I said no.

However, a good friend of mine's name was Terry Bokeno, and he was over here somewhere. They let me know that that was who they meant and that he was at Camp Carroll where he drove the tank retriever. Little

Terry driving that monster was hard to believe. I just had to see him before I left here. He was getting short, and before long he would be on his way back to the world. However, it isn't easy to just travel around like that, but perhaps there was some way I could get there. Perhaps the next day when the tankers went up there I could go with them.

One night as we were sitting around our bunker listening to the radio, everyone was set back. It was June 7 in Vietnam, and back home somewhere it was the sixth. The California primary was coming to a close. Everyone, especially I, was rooting for Bob Kennedy. If anyone could end this, it was Bob. And just about all the fighting men in Vietnam had put their trust in him when he would become our next president. As his brother, the idol of most young Americans, had done in his short term of office, Bob would carry on uniting America again.

As the announcement came over the radio, it brought me back to November 22, 1963, when the man I respected most, next to Drs. Tom Dooley and Albert Schweitzer, was shot down in the prime of his life by an assassin's bullet. John F. Kennedy was dead. I could remember it as though it were yesterday when I was sitting in a biology class taking an exam when the PA system announced that the president had been shot in Dallas. The first report said they believed he was not seriously wounded; however, Lackaye [sic], who was sitting next to me, said that this would help him in his upcoming reelection. But what if he dies? I said a little payer, hoping that he was okay, and then I tried to finish my exam, which I just couldn't manage to do.

It was Friday, and every Friday we had benediction in the auditorium. All classes were summoned to attend, and our principal, a fine man by the name of Mgsr. Cox, was on the stage. When the auditorium was filled, he told us that president John Fitzgerald Kennedy was killed in Dallas. The chills, which ran down my spine then and did so every time I thought about it, begin to recur with the announcement that another Kennedy had been struck down by an assassin's bullet. We too endured that long vigil with the rest of the nation until they said he had died from his injuries.
I could remember shaking hands with John when he was in Hype Park, New York, at the Roosevelt Estate, and I could remember shaking Bob's hand at Riverview Park in Poughkeepsie when he was running for Senator. When John was going for office, I remembered decorating my bike with

his decals and wearing his buttons constantly. And now when Bob would be running for president, I would be able to vote for him.

All our dreams about a quick end to the war seemed shattered, especially when the next day we found out that the bullet had taken its toll. Our vigil had ended. Another young Kennedy was cut down in his prime. What is this world coming to? First, John, then Martin Luther King, whom I respected for his valiant and unending efforts to obtain peace and equality among the blacks and whites of America. He had a dream, and I hope that someone with his vitality and eagerness will carry on as he would with his ever present olive branch. And after him Bob, who definitely was capable of carrying-on his brother's work. Now our nation's attention would be turned to the last remaining of the four Kennedy brothers, all of them except the youngest and surviving son, Ted, had been killed while serving America.

This and how great he and his brother were and what they were doing when John met his fate were to become a part of our everyday conversation, at least for a while. This day would never be forgotten but slipped back in our minds as the rigors of the war continued.

The day the tankers were going to Carroll, I had to go on a patrol, so I asked if they would please let him know I was here. They said they would. Perhaps he could make it up here. As we started out on the patrol, I began thinking about seeing an old buddy from back home. I could remember how we used to drink our beers up in the park when we were under age. All the good times we had were beginning to unfold in front of me. Anyway, we humped on through what I thought was the densest a jungle could be. Then we broke into a little clearing which led to the river. The current was very swift, but we waded across and proceeded on.

Once we reached the base of the Rock Pile itself, traveling was very easy. Just like walking through a field back home. Someone said he had seen a rock ape; however, he was the only one. We went around the whole base without any incidents. We could see the outpost on the very top, and as we looked at the shear sides, we thought it to be impossible for any gooks to get up there undetected; however, somehow they get up there.

Once we completed going around the base, we were off through the dense foliage. Again, our only relief was when we recrossed the river. We became self-proclaimed pathfinders in this dense undergrowth. The big knives were almost useless due to the vines, stickers, and small trees which made the countryside nearly impassable. How the gooks do it, I don't know. All the little cuts and scratches were prime targets for jungle rot, so I would be busy cleaning wounds for the next week or so.

The patrol took nearly all day, so on the way in we stopped at the bridge for a swim. It looked like a nudist camp with our squad swimming bare assed and enjoying the hell out of it while a convoy passed overhead. Seeing we were at the base camp, we decided we might as well eat here. Others started the long jump back up to Ben. While down here, we got our mail and wouldn't you know, I got my first package.

On the way back, we stopped at the mess tent. One of the fellows I had treated in the bush was working there. We managed to get all kinds of fresh fruits and canned fruits, which were the tops on all the best foods list in Vietnam. You often picked your C-rats by what kind of fruit was in it; but, now we had three gallons of fruit cocktail and two gallons of peaches, which were the preferred fruit of most. We hitched a ride with the doggies on their way up. We distributed them among the troops that night, and everyone ate well. Seeing that I had a contact in the mess hall now, we would be going down the hill almost every day.

Today, the doctor and chief of sanitation came up and jumped in my shit because the shitters weren't being burned, so I went to our squad leader asking him why they weren't being burned. And he said if I wanted them burned, that I better burn them myself. He ensured me that it was my job upon, which I clarify him of my duties. I told him that I was standing radio watch with him at night but would burn the shitters and let him stand his own watch. With this, I left and started burning the waste. Billy Bradley came up to me and asked what I was doing. I let him know that our squad leader regarded this as my duty. "He is crazy," was Bill's reply. "Go to sleep, and I'll get this, Doc." I told him I would finish; however, we both ended up doing it.

That night, he went around and told the guys that he was going to have me transferred to another platoon because, in his words, I was trying to take over the squad. When I found this out, I let him know if I were ever transferred; I would come back someday and kick the shit out of him. I wasn't about to leave my friends. The other guys in the squad said they would ask for transfers if I did leave. This made me feel real good knowing these guys would think of me so much as to stay with me. Once Cannon found out, he came back and apologized. Ever since then, we have been tight, so to speak.

My bunker was with Simmons and Landa, and after a while we decided to build a new one. We worked hard, and it looked as though we were going to have a decent hutch all underground. Another fellow, who had been with Bravo Company at Khe Sanh, had just returned. He had been in the hospital three months with ulcers supposedly, but now with about thirty days left in Vietnam he was back in the bush. Clarence Mobley was his name, and he came from South Carolina. He was a real nice guy who would do anything for you. I can remember him saying his next operation was to be his last, and then he was headed home.

Before we were to leave, we would go on one more patrol. This too was behind the Rock Pile. On the way we spotted some footprints, so we were on the lookout for anything. After walking a few hours, we decided to take five, called in our position, and found out we were resting in an old French mine field. We quickly, but carefully, vacated the area without incident. Again, we spotted some footprints by a stream, scanned the area, and headed in.

We were putting the finishing touches on our hutch when word came that we were leaving in the morning. I had to inspect all our men to make sure they were combat ready. I decided to send one man to the BAS because of his hand, which he had dropped a five-gallon water can on intentionally. He had asked me for morphine, so someone could break his hand. His mother had lost her husband recently, and there was no use losing a son, especially after they told us what to expect. I had him medevaced for a possible fracture of the wrist. I felt like sitting this one out myself.

Soon after the fellow had reached the BAS, I got a call to come down right away. I wondered, "What's the matter?" Had they found out that he did it intentionally? All of a sudden, the voice on the other end yells that it is Terry. I let him know that I was on my way down. I ran down the hill as he made his way to my pause [sic]. Just think; I would finally meet a hometown buddy and a good friend at that.

As I raced down the hill with the sweat running off me, I could see the retriever make his way toward me. When we seen each other, my arms began to waive frantically as his were. As I meet the monster, he stopped and jumped out. We slapped each other's backs for a while, and he told me how short he was, and I let him know that I practically just got here. We jumped up on the tank and headed for the BAS while talking over old times. This is truly a happy day. I was so glad he had made it down here. Then I see the guys from our hill on their tank. They said before we left they would get Terry up here one way or another, and if it meant saying something happened to their tank and they couldn't get back without assistance, then they would have to say it.

As I saw them sitting there smiling, I figured then what they did and yelled my thanks. Even if they didn't call them intentionally to come to their assistance, at least I knew that they let him know that I was here. We reminisced and talked until they had to leave. Then we said our good-byes. I told him to say hello to everyone when he got home and until then, take care, and I would do the same.

As the afternoon passed, we were busy getting ready to leave. They radioed us that our reliefs were here and to send a guide down to lead them up. Bill Bradley went as we finished packing. About half an hour later, Bill came running up in the sweltering heat to get me. On the way up, a guy from the relief column had become a heat casualty. This is a common thing in the Nam, and I was on my way. I grabbed my unit one and a few canteens of water around me and ran down to them. The guy was having some difficulties breathing, and before long we had things under control. At one point, we had to insert an airway to ensure his breathing, and the marines had remembered their first aid lessons and had taken off his shirt, began putting water on him, and had sheltered him from the sun. I called for a Jeep, which soon arrived and took our patient to the BAS. After he left, we began the long walk up the rest of the hill, which resembled a roller coaster. I grabbed some of the extra gear some fellow was humping, and then we were on our way.

Once they got sent in, we headed for the base camp. We didn't have stand lines that night, and come early morning we were headed out to an area which had known enemy activity. Rocket sites were sighted, and we were out to locate and destroy them. As the night was passing, we sat around talking of home, and it was here that I really got to know Mobley. We sat down, and he told me once he got home he was going to New York to meet a girl Flagg had told him about. "Be sure to make a stop at Lake George while there," I told him. He wouldn't regret it. He said he would. Then we talked about his stay in the hospital, and of course as everyone does, he bullshitted a little about some nurses that he had been making it with at NSA at Dang Nang.

When he took out a small container which held some pills, I asked him if I could have it once he was finished. He immediately gave it to me, putting the pills elsewhere. He asked why I wanted it, and I told him if I ever had to do a tracheotomy, it would make a pretty good airway. Little did we know the next day I would have to make use of it. Anyway, seeing it was getting late, we decided to catch some sleep. So I rolled up in a little ball on the ground and prayed for the sandman. Might as well get as much sleep as possible because tomorrow we would be humping through the bush for who knows how long.

One of the other platoon's members had decided that he wasn't going to the bush with us, however. He was a Negro named Cotton, and he had flatly told his CO that he wouldn't be going back to the bush. They could throw him in the brink if they liked, but he wasn't going back to the damn bush. Much to the disapproval of everyone else, he was given a job in the rear as our company representative at D-Med. With this, many more of his brothers would take the same means in order to evade the bush. Another guy named Dick shot himself in the foot. I guess when you make up your mind, you're not going, you just won't go no matter what measure you have to take.

June 18, 1968. We started out early in the morning being helilifted into an area which was around Cam Lo. Little did I know what this day would hold in store for me, but as we touched down, things began unfolding rapidly. The area we landed in was burning in spots where napalm had been dropped. Some of us had to jump ten to fifteen feet from the choppers, and before getting under way, we had our first casualties. A strained back suffered by one of the radio men after he was pushed from the chopper because he wouldn't jump because of seeing the chopper was too high in the air. Next was a fractured ankle. So when the next bird let its men off, he was called over to our pause [sic] for assistance.

As we regrouped and headed for our assigned positions, we could hear a firefight in the distance. Charlie Company hadn't gotten off the choppers before the gooks opened up on them. They took heavy casualties right at the beginning, which was only the start of what would be a costly day to the Ninth Marine Regiment.

Making your way cautiously forward, we stopped while they had air strikes on enemy positions. Slowly, we advanced through the bomb-scarred countryside. It was one of the hottest days I could remember, and I was lucky that I had found that fourth canteen because I would definitely be able to use it today. We advanced only meters at a time, and coming to a fairly clear area, we spotted a gook sniper. They called for a log, which is somewhat of a one-time-only bazooka. You use it, and then throw it away. Mobley got bearings on the position, however, missed slightly. Anyway, we had no trouble with him. Perhaps Mobley did get him. As we advanced further, our lead element spotted more gooks. We drew back some, and air strikes were again called in. The air show went on for about thirty minutes. At first I was watching the ARVN pilots in their World War II vintage dive bombers. It was just as you've seen in the movies; however, after a while I decided to sit back and relax while I could.

I sat down in a bomb crater with our platoon sergeant and his radioman, Joe Murphy, from Chicago. He was a real nice guy who hadn't seen his child yet but had just returned from R&R in Hawaii where he had met his wife. Also in the hole were Chicazka and a guy named Hannel, who had been in Vietnam on his second tour for only a week. He was a squad leader and was asking Sgt. Buchanan what the scoop was. After a while, Mobley came up and sat next to me saying he was too short to die, so he thought he would like to share our protection. As he sat next to me, I continued to read *Rosemary's Baby*. The crater was filled with its six soon-to-be victims, and after about five minutes, someone yelled, "What was that?" Disregarding my book for a moment, I looked up, and then all hell broke loose. I was thrown back unconscious for a few seconds, and as the area began clearing, I could see the craters and its victims lying in pools of their blood. The stench of warm blood flooded the area and was nauseating.

Soon, everyone was yelling for a corpsman. Pleas for "Al. Doc, help me," began to smother my senses and made me so very uncertain that I could do anything for them. It seemed to go on for hours, but I quickly snapped out of the daze and began treating the men. First, I turned to Mobley next to me. As far as I could tell, a piece of shrapnel had cut his aorta, and within a few seconds he would be dead. Blood was already streaming from his mouth and nose. He also had a shrapnel hole below the eye that undoubtedly entered his brain.

It wasn't five minutes ago he had said he was too short to die, but now his challenge to death was met and he lost. I yelled for more corpsmen while distributing battle dressings to Flagg and Terry Landa who had come to help me patch up the wounded. As I wiped the blood from my face, I got up to move to Hannel but fell. I hadn't noticed or felt the shrapnel wounds on my legs in the excitement. Spitting out more blood and chips of teeth, I pulled myself toward Hannel who was screaming in pain. Dragging myself past Chicazka, I noticed that he had had his radial artery cut. I told him to put his finger in the hole until I could help him. Believe it or not, it helped control his loss of blood.

The squad leader had to be treated first and upon reaching him, I tried to keep him quiet. His body was completely riddled with shrapnel, and as I placed a tourniquet on the right arm, I began a human albumin injection in his left arm. Human albumin is a blood volume expander, and he needed it. I was sure glad that I had carried those extra two bottles. When I picked up his arm, I actually thought it was going to come off in my hand, it was so badly mangled. Besides his arm, his legs and abdomen were filled with shrapnel wounds, but hopefully he would make it if we got him out in time. Help was arriving and I reassured the guys everything was okay.

As we continued our work, the tubes popped again. Everyone ran out, leaving the wounded. Seeing I had Hannel's flak jacket off, I laid over him, shielding him with my body. He was bad enough now without sustaining any more wounds. "Come on, Doc. Get out of there. They have the place zeroed in," was all I could hear, except for the tubes. With this, the other guys began to yell for someone to get them out. I reassured them that lightening doesn't strike twice in the same spot; at least I prayed it wouldn't. It's those few tense moments which seem like eternity from when you hear the tubes pop, and when they land, that really is mind bending. All you have ever done or ever hoped to do passes in front of your mind within seconds. You also wonder just how close to you it will land this time.

After the explosion, you are relieved, but only until the tubes pop again. As the rounds landed on the lip of the crater, I pleaded with God to have them stop. "Please, Lord, they had enough," was all I could say. As the ground cleared, help returned. As we continued to treat them, the tubes popped again and again, with each shot being further away but not a whole hell of a lot. When we finished treating the guys, we sent them to the LZ, which is the Landing Zone, to be medevaced out. I told the guys to take Hannel as I moved to Sgt. B. I knew he would have to be trached, but our senior corpsman said no; I would have to come back to him because others of the world had a better chance of living.

Chicazka had sustained extensive shrapnel wounds but would be okay. I bandaged him up, and he too was taken to the LZ afterward. By this time, everyone was out of the crater except Murphy. When they said, "What's that?" Joe had laid on his belly, and it's a good thing because all his wounds were in his rear. Some spinal injury was expected because he could not move his legs. He would have an exploratory laporandony [sic] once he got to the hospital, but he would be all right in time. We finished bandaging him and began to carry him to the LZ, me hopping along on one leg while carrying my part of the man-made stretcher.

As we were going along, I heard a cry for a corpsman again, and I knew it must be the sergeant. I half ran, half hopped to the origin of the plea and just as I expected, Sgt. B, was convulsing. I dropped his head back and slit his throat as they showed us in the movies on how to perform a tracheotomy. I inserted an airway, the same one that Mobley had given me the night before in case I ever had to do a trach. The sergeant had half his face taken off, and some of the jaw bone had lodged in his throat. Poor Mobley would never know.

Anyway, by this time he was clinically dead. He wasn't breathing, and his heart had stopped. I did mouth-to-mouth airway and close cardiac massage for a while, and then he began maintaining his own. The airway was a little large, so I grabbed a ballpoint pen and broke off part of the end after unscrewing one half and inserting it into his trachea. It worked like it was made to order, and his respirations and pulse remain constant after sucking the blood clot for his throat.

Once we got to the LZ, I asked the signal man where the chopper was to land, so we could be on as quickly as possible. When he said he didn't know yet, I asked what the hell he was waiting for. Soon thereafter, we had our LZ, and I told which guys to take and in what order. By this time, the guys were trying to treat me, but I said no, I was too busy. I soon would be at a hospital. When the bird landed, everything went smoothly, thanks to the great guys in our platoon. Barney became my support as I went around checking on everyone. And when the bird came in, he hurried me there to make sure I didn't miss it. "Thanks, Barney, and be careful," were my departing words, though he couldn't hear me over the wail of the chopper blades as he and Jim threw me aboard.

We made it off the ground and were headed for D-Med, which is at Dong Ha. En routed the sergeant cut short on life again, but was quickly revived. As we touched down and were carried to triage, I let the doctors know what had been done. By this time, they began checking my wounds. I had a hole in my cheek, and they were worried that I had a fractured mandible. Also, I had what looked like a half inch nail in my right shoulder which I pulled out. They dressed that and the three holes in my leg and face, then sent me to the Air Force transit where I would get a flight to Phu Bai. I was helped down the corridor, which in time I would get to know quite well because little did I know that in another six months I would be working here.

While waiting, they brought in Czaika and Murphy. Hannel went to surgery and Sgt. B was going to the ship. I hope they all make it. Bandit and DJ, who were in the rear, came to see us, as well as our top sergeant. They reassured us everything was okay now. We arrived at D-Med at 1315, which I would look up some eight months later while on duty there. We never arrived at Phu Bai until 11:30 that night. I can remember Joe and Czaika thanking me, and I also could remember me wishing my leg was broken, so I could get the hell out of Vietnam.

Mobley lost his challenge with death and died twenty-eight days before he was to rotate back to the world. Czaika and Murphy would go to Japan. And Hassle lost his arm and would go back to the states. Sgt. Buchanan lived on borrowed time and died on the hospital ship, the USS *Sanctuary*, which I found out after I returned to my unit, which would be more than a month from now.

Once we got to Phu Bai on a medevac flight of twenty-five guys, five of whom were corpsmen; our wounds were to be treated. On the way, I met some of the familiar faces of the first platoon who had run into the firefight as soon as they landed. Johnson, who was on his second tour of duty and a cousin of White, who was to be our squad leader in time, had caught a bullet in the head. He would be dead by morning, unfortunately. Perhaps, just like Sgt. B, this would be best because if he had lived, he would have been a vegetable due to the extent of his injuries. Anyway, I was sent to x-ray and to S and D (surgery and debridement). A fellow corpsman helped me along, asked if I needed anything. Yes, I did. I needed some water. They would not give us any because we might have to go to surgery. So we made our way to the water fountain with cold water, and I just made a lush of myself. It was like a little bit of heaven. After I had my fill, we went to S and D to have my wounds debrided.

The doctor was a fellow New Yorker. He took a little time and seventeen sutures to close the wound inside and outside of my mouth. He couldn't get two little pieces of shrapnel, however, and left them. Moving to my leg was next. His finger traveled the route of the shrapnel, and I let out a scream. "What the fuck are you doing, Doc?" As I turned to one side, I seen a chaplain standing there, and I apologized for cursing. Then I seen a sign which said, "Pain builds character" and sort of laughed to myself in order to distract myself from what the doctor was doing, another way to brainwash the marines. I had to try harder not to yell, which I did accomplish. The shrapnel was so far in that they decided to leave it in also. They packed the hole with what seemed to be an endless piece of gauze, then dressed it and moved to my knee. After removing the shrapnel, they packed this also, dressed it, and sent me to a ward. I thanked them as I was wheeled out in a chair. Upon reaching the ward, I was greeted by a corpsman who had been with us in 1/9 and for a while was our senior corpsman. I related the activities of the day as I lay in bed.

After he left, I lay there awake all night hoping everyone else was okay. I prayed for Mobley and cried a little because there was nothing I could do for him. He was the first man I had ever seen get killed, and he was sitting right next to me when it happened. He died in my lap. He didn't belong there; but, if he hadn't, perhaps I would have been killed. I guess that's the way God had it planned. I couldn't believe how I lucked out after everyone else was hurt so badly. If I hadn't looked up when I did, I probably would have lost an eye. Thinking of how lucky I was, I thanked God. I finally realized just how great life is, especially after seeing someone lose his and helping others to maintain theirs. Being a corpsman had given me the opportunity to do this, and now I have the greatest love and respect for life, and hopefully these ideals of life will always be my guidelines.

June 19, 1968.

Getting out of bed early, I gathered my crutches and made it to the admissions section of the hospital in order to find out where Murphy and Czaika had gone. I found out and made it to the Intensive Care Unit where Joe was. Upon arriving last night, they took him to surgery where he underwent emergency exploratory laparotomy to find out if any internal damage was sustained. He was awake smiling when I walked in. "Hi ya, Doc" sounded so good. Good to know that we were out of the bush and still alive. I asked how he felt, saying he looked great, even with all his tubes in place. He reassured me he was fine. And I told him Czaika had been sent to Dang Nang last night, and I was leaving in an hour or so. We said our good-byes and told each other we would keep in touch. However, little did I know we would never see each other again, at least while in the Nam, because before long Joe would be sent to Japan and later on to the U.S.

As our departure time came around, I made it to our designated area. It was here that I met John Orazabal, whom I would become great friends within the next month or so. The big Texan helped me with my gear as I walked to the plane. We were headed for an Air Force hospital in Da Nang. We would remain here for a few days, and then we were off to Cam Ranh Bay, which proved to be a vacation land for us. While in Da Nang, I finished reading *Rosemary's Baby* which I found on a shelf and thought of the hell we were just through, especially the other guys.

Also while at Da Nang, I was to run into Cink, who had shot himself in the foot with a .45 pistol the night before the operation while at the Rock Pile. He later told me he had done it purposefully to avoid going on the op, which I couldn't blame him for. After all, being eighteen is just the beginning of life, and why should we throw it away in a land where we didn't belong, at least in the capacity that we were there in. He too would be going to Cam Ranh Bay with us and later on to Japan. He didn't belong in Nam anyway. Anyone who would deliberately wound himself didn't belong in the bush because he could cause injuries to someone else.

When we left for Cam Ranh Bay, I became a little impatient because I was ordered not to walk. Being carried around made me feel so useless, and I could hardly wait to get up and around again. My stay at Cam Ranh Bay would prove very interesting, and the guys I was to meet I would never forget. They loaded us on the ambulance bus taking us to the airstrip. They then loaded us about four high in the belly of a giant medevac plane, and before we knew it, we were airborne. Once landed at Cam Ranh Bay, we again were put into ambulance buses and headed toward the hospital.

On the way to the hospital, we passed some Vietnamese working on the base. The driver, who was an Air Force member and who hadn't seen any action undoubtedly here said how he would like to throw a frag into a truckload of gooks as we were passing them. It was filled with old men, women and children, but this hard ass wanted to kill them for no reason. Perhaps he was saying it because he figured that's the way we felt.

On the contrary, because I wasn't the only one who asked him what the hell was wrong with him. A few guys laughed, but for the most part everyone wanted to know what his problem was. It's guys like this, if he was for real that destroy by their ignorance all we have accomplished with our hardships and some of their lives. I had seen the disrespect for the people before and in the future would see it again and again, hard-ass—or should we say hardheaded marines throwing cans of food at kids trying to hit them. In the future, I would be treating many such victims, as well as kids, hit by trucks and even a tank.

Anyway, we are now at the hospital. We were carried into their triage, and according to the nature of your injuries, it would be determined if you remained here or went on to Japan. At first I was to go to Japan, but they changed their minds and let me stay. Thanks a lot. I was sent to Ward 9 with "Oddjob" as we called Orazabela because he was the only one of our group who could get around. I was to remain in bed for a week, and then graduated to a wheelchair. My face was swollen up on the left side where it looked as if I had a soft handball in my mouth, and besides changing and packing my leg wounds three times a day, the doctor also struck me with a needle every morning to aspirate the blood clotting in my cheek. I think I dreaded that the most. [can't read]

As the days went by, we began to form a close-knit group who, besides Oddjob from Houston, Texas, and had been wounded the same day as I, included his corpsman, Craig Welch. Craig, who came from Lima, Ohio, had been wounded in the arm. They had gotten hit pretty hard, and to top that, our own bombers hit them. It seems as though there was a fire by the landing zone. Hidden in the grass was a red flare, which caught on fire and released a little signal of red smoke, which generally is used to point out the position of the enemy. The jet came screaming down on our American men, who had already been wounded and were waiting to be medevaced out. According to his calculations, nine men were killed and another twelve injured. I would meet Craig again before my tour of duty was completed and would again meet him at my next duty station back in the world.

Next there was La Val Van Etten from the Fifth Marines. His point man had stepped on a booby trap and was killed, along with the man behind him. Van was about six men back and managed to catch a large piece in the thigh. He came from upstate New York not far from me, and we made plans to meet again once we got home.

After him came another corpsman who had went to school with Craig and also was from Lima, Ohio. Bill Zimmerman was his name, and he was unfortunate enough to have gotten malaria. I would see him too before I left the Nam. As matter of fact, we would have a party at the hospital I worked in before he left. After my tour in the bush was completed, he too would be going to Great Lakes Naval Hospital upon his rotation and would leave Vietnam with me.

The guy from Connecticut was next. Barry Masterson was the name, and he came from Thompsonville. At the time he was in the hospital with an abscess, but seven days before he was to rotate, he was to be wounded. One week to go and the gooks attacked their cap unit. First, he was hit with an AK-47 round in the belly, and as the battle progressed; he was to get hit again with shrapnel from a mortar round impacting nearby. He was awarded the Bronze Star and two Purple Hearts for that night, but it was costly. He would be partly paralyzed on one side for the rest of his life; however, he was getting his discharge from the service soon. Something just about every man looks forward to.

Fields was next and the last of our usual group. He came from Georgia, and everyone called him "Strawberry" after the then popular song of "Strawberry Fields." He would do anything for a laugh. He had just received his third heart and was headed home. His girl was waiting to get married once he got home, at least he thought so, but in time would find out different.

This concluded the "Notorious Seven" in Ward 9, and the week to come would prove to be a memorable one. Every morning we woke to the orders of a gunny sergeant from the Army who had caught a few pieces of shrapnel in the leg. When he got up he woke everyone else to do their morning chores of sweeping, mopping, and the general cleanliness of the ward. While this was going on, I laid back catching a few extra winks. At times I prepared myself for the doctor's rounds. Today, I was going to ask him if I could get out of bed.

When he came around I asked him, and he let me up only in a wheelchair. At least that's a step. As soon as I could, I got a wheelchair and made my way outside with Oddjob pushing me along. I found out that they had a Vietnamese ward on my tour of the grounds. I could see the little kids in there. Boy, how would I like to work there. As we went around observing the air, we could see the natives sweeping, working in the chow hall, cleaning the laundry and what not, and they all seemed to be smiling. Perhaps a pseudo smile, but to me they seemed to be authentic. And I felt comfortable around them. We found out how to say hello in Vietnamese, and as we passed a gook, we would say "chow," which seemed to please them.

Most of the afternoon was spent outside in the warm air, and the nights were spent in the Red Cross building where they had a movie most nights and a USO show once or twice a week. One day, I met Woody Hayes, the coach for the Ohio State Buckeyes and another time had the pleasure of meeting Joyce Tyleson and Pat Morrow, two actresses from the "Peyton Place" show. They talked with us for about half an hour despite the plea from their guide to leave. It really made you feel good knowing that the people, some of the people back in the world are still behind you. My twenty-first birthday was a day I will never forget, besides the fact that I had to spend it in Vietnam. We had a USO show, and all wheelchairs were up front BAT, and I was enjoying the show as we could be picturing ourselves sitting there in wheelchair, legs wrapped and my face swollen, but sure enjoyed the girls. One was an Italian girl from New Jersey, and she reminded me so much of Lynne. What a doll.

God, why couldn't I be home? Anyway, as the show progressed, she sang a song just for me. "You're' just too good to be true. Can't take my eyes off of you" were repeated mentally many a times in the next few months and served to raise my spirits while bringing back those memories while a patient at Cam Ranh Bay. It all seemed so unreal that we were in a war-torn country, yet being entertained by a couple of American girls who could put your heart and mind back home. I almost felt it was worthwhile getting hit. At least I was out of the bush, and I hoped I would never go back.

My first letter came from my folks who were worried sick; but, the next night I surprised them with a phone call. It was known as a Mars call and was relayed over a radio. Every time you finished a sentence, you would say "Over," and then your party would answer, and then when he finished he too would reply with "Over." My mother was so startled that she could hardly talk. And as for myself, I was so choked up that the words came out barely audible. However, it was really great talking to them and made you feel that much closer to home.

My first letter from Lynne arrived the next morning, and it made me feel good to know she was really worried about my welfare. Her and her mother sat there crying when she was informed about my injuries. After being wounded, I wrote my parents the first available moment and asked them to replay the message to Lynne, letting her know I was fine. The next chance I got, I would write to Lynne. They had received the letter the same day the state department informed them of my injuries and telephoned Lynne, who had a letter waiting when she arrived home from work and was greeted by her mother with the news of my becoming a statistic of the war. All she wanted was to be there with me, so she could take care of my injuries. I too wished she were here; better yet, me there.

In one of the bunches of letters, there was one from Jackie and Jimmie. They were Joe's sister and brother-in-law and a great couple. I envied them at times, and I wished my marriage would be as lovely as theirs. Jim had offered to loan me the money to go to school rather than go into the service. However, I realized that I wasn't ready to settle down and do some serious studying, so I joined. Now I wished I hadn't because sure as hell I wouldn't be in the mess I'm in now.

Being around July 4, Jim wanted me to thank all the guys who were over here fighting in order that he could enjoy the annual family picnic back home, and so his children could do likewise in the future. He was really proud of the young men doing their duty in Vietnam and wanted to be certain that we knew it. That letter was passed through many hands since then. He also stated how Little Jimmy had waken one night and was wondering where I was. The next night he woke again and said that there was something wrong with me, and his mother reassured him I was fine. A few days later, however, she found out that there was something wrong with me. Perhaps Little Jimmy has some ESP powers. If so, right then I would like to find out from him if I would indeed make it home safely.

While laid up in bed, particle jokes became one of our favorite pastimes. Often, I was behind them. One time in particular, we had bandaged Strawberry's head and told him to complain of excessive pain in his head. To put on a good show, he hollered to the corpsmen to get a nurse quickly, he couldn't stand it any longer. Upon her arrival, Strawberry began to tell her of the surgery he had had, and it was now bothering him something terrible. He indeed had had surgery, but it was on his arm, not on his head. She quickly asked about his head to which he replied how he had had a hysterectomy that day. As she flushed, everyone else on the ward had busted up. She too began to laugh while departing, stopping at my bed to ask if I had put him up to that. Who me?

Every night after I was up and around, we first went to the show and then sat behind our ward singing folk songs such as "Where Have All the Flowers Gone?" "Gone to hippies, everyone" soon became our reply. I wouldn't mind being a hippy myself, but not the pseudo hippy who is just conforming to nonconformism. One, who really believes in love, is dedicated to the services of others, more compassionate, more responsible to himself and the feelings of others, and one who is more practical in certain aspects of life. He is the true hippy. One who knows that violence is a tool of the ignorant and realizes that the only way to accomplish something worthwhile is by good example or any means that is peaceful. This is my line, after all what has riots [can't read] campus disorders accomplish, except spreading hate and discontent among all those involved? Nothing. Even cost the lives of students at Kent and Jackson State.

People must be able to get along with everyone else in order to obtain the smallest of goals. If people could only learn to cooperate with one another, what a wonderful world this could be. Just think, no more war, no more senseless killings, and no more unnecessary sorrows. What if they gave a war and nobody came? Then indeed we have accomplished something here on earth.

Even in Nam, we need more understanding between ourselves and the Vietnamese. Perhaps if we had that understanding, there would never have been Maj Lo or the death of sixteen civilians by a marine patrol. Perhaps a student wouldn't have died in Qui Nhon giving cause of unrest to other students who are opposed to our presence in their homeland. Perhaps with a little understanding that last child to receive a fractured skull from a can of C-rats being thrown off the truck would not have sustained that injury. Perhaps most significant of all with understanding, the people would be on our side and see what we are trying to do for them, and then maybe the war could be done a little quicker. Unfortunately, we do not have this understanding.

Seeing I was up and around, they put me to work changing dressings, and for my last two weeks, I did the suturing on our ward. It was a challenge just to see how good a job I could do. One particular day, a fellow named Hopper was to be sewed up. He had sustained superficial shrapnel wounds of the belly and one massive wound where a piece of shrapnel had traveled between his arm and chest just beneath his armpit. The wound was extensive, and after considerable debriding and underlining, the wound was ready to be sewn. I was instructing the Air Force corpsmen, showing the proper sterile techniques that should be employed. Masterson was my assistant, and we did a beautiful job of minimizing the scar area. On my last operation, I met Hopper again, and all he could say was that it didn't leave a big enough scar. Typical of a marine.

We now made our way to the beach every day. I wasn't supposed to leave the ward but could hardly resist. The water was crystal clear and reminded me of Freeport in the Bahamas. At the beach they sold cold beer, sodas, hot dogs, hamburgers just like you were back home. Also a jukebox played all the latest hits. Upon making it back to the ward, I would clean and dress my wounds. The doctor marveled how clean my wounds looked; however, he couldn't understand how come it was taking so long to heal. Little did he realize what my daily activities consisted of, and it was beneficial to me that he never found out. Taking pictures became a daily habit and served to remind us of the good times we had experienced while recovering from war injuries.

We soon would be leaving the hospital and going back to our units, something I was not looking forward to. I wouldn't get back to them until the last of July, which meant that I had been out of action for nearly a month and a half. Oddjob, Craig, Bat, Bill, and I were all discharged. I never did score on Donna, one of the Air Force nurses who had taken care of me, though I sure would have liked to. Guess I just wanted to save it all for Lynne. Anyway, where could I go with hospital PJ on and not be noticed. Donna had managed to lose my discharge papers for a few days, but now it was time to leave this haven and become a grunt again.

All my friends were leaving, so what the hell. We all were booked on a flight to Dang Nang; however, not until we had one last barb together. We had managed to get into the EM Club and thoroughly enjoyed ourselves. When we finally reached Dang Nang, we said good-bye to each other and reminded all to keep in touch. We had planned to meet each other in Lake George, New York, in two years; however, things like that never worked out.

Again, I was at the III MAF Terminal where I had seen them unloading the dead cargo of twenty-five bodies on my first day in Vietnam. The wait was short, and before long I had landed in Dong Ha where our rear had been located. Upon reaching the area, I found it deserted except for a few guys who were cleaning up. I walked into a hutch where there was some activity and asked where there was some activity and asked the red-headed guy behind the desk, "Hey, man. Do you know where 1/9 moved to?" With this, some lifer jumped in my shit because I hadn't said "sir." How was I to know that the whippy character behind the desk was a lieutenant? If he wants to be addressed as "sir," he should wear his bars. With this I left and asked someone with a little more intelligence and tact where 1/9's new area was located. The private had told me they moved to Quang Tri after the ammo dump blew up. I thanked him and hitchhiked my way to Quang Tri.

After much searching, I reached our rear area which was only tents but definitely better than sleeping on the ground in the bush. I would have to get used to sleeping on the ground again after the luxury of a nice, soft hospital bed, but why rush it. Upon reaching our area, I received a warm welcome and met another corpsman who had been stationed with me at Jacksonville, Florida. Jim Hitchman was his name, and he had just gotten wounded the day before. After a few days, he would be back in action with the wounds in his arm healed. Also, forty-six letters and six packages were waiting for me; letters from people I had went to school with, people who knew my folks or who knew me from work. I would never hear from them a second time unless I was to get hit again, probably. The small pile from Lynne were saved to last and if things went right, in nine months I would be going home and maybe getting married.

On the way to the mess hall, I came across Bob Shuman who had been in field medical service school with me. He came from Massachusetts and was now working with 3/9. While in the rear I would be spending a lot of time with him on July 29.

I heard the guys were coming in off an operation today, so I said the hell with the two weeks in the rear. I didn't need convalescence leave anyway. I had all my gear reissued and caught the first convoy to LZ Stud (Vandergrift Combat Base). I just had to get back after finding out that they wanted to decorate me. Deep down inside it makes you feel great knowing that the guys appreciate what you did. On the way, I would have plenty of candy to pass out to the kids from my packages, and I was glad that I could share it with them and bring a little happiness to their shattered lives.

As we passed through Cam Lo refugee village, I could see the kids lined up on the road and began distributing the candy among those wretched little kids who had nothing but a smile as payment. It was enough. Some of the guys were throwing some extra C-rat cans to the hungry children, but there was always an ass in the group who has to use the children as targets. What have they done to him? This guy had just arrived, and I let him know that that was enough. If he didn't stop, I would inform the convoy officer. He heeded my warning and helped me distribute some gum and candy. After all, deliberate and crude acts such as this will turn the people away from our pacification programs. This was something we didn't need. These people remember things like this, and instead of putting their trust in our hands, they will fall to the VC and NVA even more so than they are now.

Upon reaching Stud, I was directed toward the area 1/9 had just settled in. They had just arrived from the bush and were setting up a bivouac area for the night. I could feel the tension in my body soar as I approached their area. First, I had to pass through Charlie Co. where Sibe was the first to greet me, along with a beer warm, but nonetheless a beer. He pointed out our area, and I proceeded on. Paul Flagg was the first recognizable face I encountered. He looked up as his pupils dilated to get what seemed to be a better look and yelled, "The Doc is back." Heads began popping up as some began running toward me. Some slapped my back while others shook my hand and began taking my gear. It was a welcoming sight to see all the guys and know they were okay and tears of joy escaped me.

Jim Simmons, after his warm welcome, gave me all of Lynne's letters I carried up to the day I was wounded. He had faithfully carried them because he knew how much they meant to me. Upon reaching the unit, however, I found out that another corpsman had taken my place. Everyone wanted to know if I was coming back, and I reassured them I was. Billy, Wolf, Outlaw, Barney, Terry, Jim, and Flagg were all right, and new faces appeared after DJ and Dave had left. Making my way to the CP, I ran across Jim that the other corpsman had friends in the third squad, so if he wanted, I would trade with him. After he said okay, I informed the other corpsmen that he was going to the third squad, and I was to bring him over right away. I helped him with his gear and introduced him to the members of the third squad that I had known. After that was over, I settled down with my old buddies.

That night with Steve's care package from home and mine, we ate well, and the next day we moved to man the lines at Stud. We were to be there for some time, and actually we hoped we would remain here for the duration of the monsoon season. Once we got set in, I was off to meet the new faces.

While I was away, we got a new platoon commander whose name just happened to be Myers. We got to know each other fairly well, especially seeing we were always looking for one another because we had received the other's mail. He came from Amtracks, after our other leuy was killed in July. Glad I missed that day. Five guys killed just in one hole. After a job well done with 1/9, he would return to Amtraks. Also in the platoon was a new sergeant named Chapman who was grungy as hell but was well respected, especially after he had gotten us off Slaughter Ridge in August. After meeting them, I returned to my squad and had a long talk with Jim "Slippery" Sloan, who I had met the night before. He quickly became known as Red and hailed from Lily, Pennsylvania. He would relate many amusing tale about him and his girl Pat in the next few months and proved to be a big morale booster for the squad.

Next came Frank Van NuyHuyes, whom I didn't fare out too well with. He was a know-it-all jar head from the beginning, who deemed himself infallible. He had come from Junior's hometown of Marietta, Georgia, and they, needless to say, were the best of buddies. It's good to have some part of home with you when you're over here, even if it's just a guy from the same state. Hamilton, who had been with 1/9 at Khe Sanh and wounded there, was sent to Japan to heal his wounds and had just returned to the unit. In a few months, he would be going back to the world, but only for thirty days. He would then come back as an MP in Dang Nang. Rest assured once I get home, there is no way in hell I was coming back.

Also, White was now our squad leader. It was his cousin who was killed on June 18, after returning to the Nam after once being seriously wounded. It only took him two weeks on his second tour to make it home in a box with a flag draped over it. Both these guys were colored but never held a match to Billy.

The second squad also had new men, one being a fellow named Moren from Connecticut, who in time I would pull from under a mule at Ca Lu. He was a very generous and thoughtful guy but wasn't liked as well as he should have been. He had just arrived at the company and already was the CO driver, was going back to Oki for a school, and when in the bush, he stayed with the CP. It was said that his parents were very well-off and that his luck was overtones of this; however, to me he was a swell guy, a good trooper, and one who just happened to be in the right place at the right time. He knew people in Highland, New York, right across the river from me, and someday we hoped to meet each other again.

Tigue, who came from California, soon became my contact in the mess hall, seeing Sugarbear, my previous contact, was going home after writing to his Congressman telling him he wasn't getting proper medical care over here.

We would stay here at Stud not for the duration of the monsoons, but until the sixteenth of August when we would participate in an operation which would separate the men from the boys. However, in our platoon there were no boys. While at Stud, we would get warm food at least once a day, mail came regularly, and there was a shower every day if you wanted to walk the mile. Most of the days were filled by improving our bunkers and playing Back Alley Bridge of which I became quite a player. Occasionally, there would be a patrol, and all we did most of the time was get far enough out of sight, set up a watch, and relax for a few hours. The letters kept coming from Lynne, but Wolfe was still waiting for the day they would stop. I knew they wouldn't.

Somewhere around the sixth of August, we got a new trooper named Joseph Arnold. A cocky SOB he was and hailed from Warsaw, Indiana. In time, he would be one of the guys who would help carry on the name and reputation of 1/9 as so many brave men had in the past. He was an asthmatic and really didn't belong in the bush; however, once we got back, I was going to see if we could keep him from going in the bush. His first attack was shortly after he arrived.

We were still manning the lines at Stud, and I called for a Jeep. Two hours later, it arrives. His attack had ceased. They told him a doctor had to witness the attack in order to get out of the bush. At a later date, he would suffer a severe attack and would be medevaced from the bush. Damn near cost him his life. And from there, he would be medevaced back to the world where I would eventually meet him at the Great Lakes Naval Hospital. At one time during our tour, I would prevent him from falling out of a chopper, something we would both remember. After Andy—Moses as he was also known—lost his cockiness, we became the best of friends.

Sick call and passing out of our anti-malaria pills were carried out on a daily schedule. This was done faithfully because of the increase lately of malaria among the troop of the Third Marine Division. All dental work and pressing business in the rear was taken care of as we took advantage of our extra leisure time. Red and I would stop by the food dump daily after our shower and steal a case of C-rats when possible or make it to our mess area where I was able to get a gallon or two of fruit. Little did we know that this was the lull before the storm. We had actually thought we would be staying at Stud for the monsoons, especially since we started digging trenches from bunker to bunker, which served as our drainage system.

When August 16 arrived, we packed up and began moving out. Going on a.m. operation which was to begin at Con Thien and end up taking us to Chopper Valley (also named because of the number of choppers shot down over the area), which is a stone's throw from the DMZ. We packed our belongings sadly and made our way to the airstrip, knowing that someone else would now settle for good at Stud while we humped through the bush. The rain began, and we were off. August 16, we waited at the strip for the choppers, and as they landed, we scurried to them. They would be taking us within seeing distance of Con Thien, our northern most outpost.

Like always, our squad managed to get on the first wave of choppers which was much to our disliking. Upon landing, we hurried to find any available protection. I had managed to conceal most of myself under some brush but was more than I had bargained for because when the next wave of choppers approached, one almost landed on me. I rolled over on my back and began waving my arms frantically in order to capture the pilot's attention. Upon noticing me, he pulled away a little. I still could have extended my leg and kicked the damn wheel. When it finally landed, Junior looked up in disbelief, seeing the wheel settle down right next to him. Be a hell of a way going home and trying to explain how you were injured in Nam. "Got hit by a chopper." Who would believe that? Everyone had touched down, and we fanned out, taking up our previously plotted positions. To our right was Con Thien, a frequent target of the enemies as they crossed the DMZ.

Things were quiet for the first few days as we watched air strikes hit the valley, which was across the plain which extended in front of us. They were continuous for nearly three days with B-52 strikes hitting around Con Thien. I was taking pictures with my Instamatic of the air strikes when in the sky; I could see a plane which looked as though it was going to go for a strike. What a picture. All of a sudden, it burst into flames, and within seconds, it was burning fiercely on the ground. An antiaircraft gun had found its mark, but the pilots had managed to eject. I hope they weren't hurt any. Imagine how they felt as they drifted down into enemy territory.

Luckily, two gunships and helicopters were in the immediate area and went in and picked up the two men quickly. At least I assume they got them. The chopper seemed to stay on the ground for an eternity, but they were up and away leaving behind them the pilot's burning craft that had been a $2 million investment of the American people.

As the fourth night came around, things got a little bit jumpy when Frank thought he heard someone. I was on watch two holes away and I thought I heard it too, so I woke Red right away. After waking him, I got into the foxhole and nearly broke my neck doing so, after finding out how deep Red had dug it. The gooks were out there playing tricks on our minds trying to have us give our positions away. However, we were expecting that and instead of firing at them, Frank threw a few frags. It sounded as though they were out there with a can tied to the end of a piece of string, dragging it behind them at a safe distance. Word was passed from our CP that if another frag was thrown, we had better drag in a body come morning.

I spent most of the night awake and wondering what would be next. Nothing did and when morning came we checked the area, finding nothing. We were sent out on a patrol of the area, which was cut short when they told us to return. We were moving out. Walking most of the day, we set in and waited. Apparently this had been a position held by the gooks long ago because we had found some of their equipment, as well as a couple of skeletons. While walking we had passed the place where Jay Johnson had had heat stroke back in July. Damn near died while I was taking it easy in the hospital. Anyway, he pulled through. Doc Barb had taken care of him and did a fine job getting Jay breathing again. I would soon find out that Doc Barb had died of malaria. I never got the chance to thank him for taking care of my guys while I was away. Now he knows how I feel. So, Doc, thank you. Those guys mean a hell of a lot to me.

Things were easy here after we dug in and on the twenty-second we were to move out early. About six o'clock the choppers came and we were headed to Chopper Valley. As we hurried off the choppers, we immediately spread out checking the area because we had been landed on the wrong hill. Two hills over was our original destination; however, we would use this new area for our base camp. We dug our holes and as we were sitting around to see what was to happen, someone yelled for us to "Break up the mob down there." It was only our squad picking C-rats. Everyone looked up to see who was doing the yelling. He was barely visible with his pack of men around him, but when he yelled again, I asked why he didn't practice what he was preaching. Of course a smile accompanied the remark.

The next word was "Hey, Marine, wipe that smile off your face." I knew damn well it was me he was talking to, but I looked around anyway when he said, "You, the one with the gray t-shirt on." I turned to him and let him know that I wasn't a marine. His reply was then I didn't belong out here, which I assured him he was correct and to see if he could tell the guys in the rear the same. I've been trying to tell them that since I got here.

His next statement was so trite to that; the squad had all they could do to keep from laughing in the idiot's face. He asked how I dare talk to him like that. "I'll have you know that I'm a sergeant in the U.S. Marine Corps and furthermore, I'm platoon commander for the Fourth Platoon." Just to show him how much it meant to me, my reply was that my mother didn't smoke. He said he didn't give a shit if my mother smoked grass. And I told him I didn't give a shit if he was a sergeant in the USMC. With this some splib [sic] dude jumped up and said, "Let me get him, Sergeant. I'll take care of him." I let it be known that he wasn't getting any brownie points for his little show, so he might just as well sit down. I then sat down and began eating my C-rats. I'm not generally a hard ass, but I guess I was just letting some tension off. Perhaps it was because I hadn't gotten a letter from Lynne in three days now. They must be tied up somewhere. After all, Woffe can't be right.

By ten o'clock that morning, we were headed out. We were going to scout out the area and end up on the hill where we were suppose to land to begin with. Little did we know what lies ahead, and when we finally made it back late on the night of the twenty-third of August, that splib [sic] dude who wanted to take care of me was one of the first guys to welcome me back and greet me with a canteen of cool water, something I hadn't had for damn near two days.

Our platoon was to go to the hill we were to land on and check out the area. As they moved down a fairly recently-traveled trail, they encountered a hill which had undoubtedly seen quite a bit of action in the past. Our squad was to stand by on the hill while the other two squads proceeded on. We settled on the hill with the painful reminders of war scattered about. U.S. flak jackets, helmets, and parts of rifles were all about the area. Hanging in a tree was a flak jacket and helmet, which gave an eerie feeling of death lingering in the air. I cut it down and then sat on the side of the hill checking the remains of an M-16 rifle. Wonder what is happening ahead.

Like the touching down of a sudden tornado, all hell broke loose. Up ahead the area which had been prepped with arty, the gooks had opened up on the other two squads. Immediately we took cover, and it was here that instincts paid out. While opening up on them with automatic and small arms fire, they let mortars rain into our position. On the far side of the hill, someone yelled for a doctor, and I was off on what was to be the beginning of a busy day. There on the other side of the hill was another platoon which had been sent out as security for us after they had spotted some gooks on the adjoining hill. I asked who was calling for the corpsman.

The squad leader was talking to a new grunt who got sort of shell shocked when the fireworks began. As I was recrossing the hill back to my squad, two more rounds went off; and I caught a small piece of shrapnel, it got me in the wrist. Nothing to worry about, thank God. I don't know how none of our guys didn't get hit because Junior and Hennington were headed right toward me when the round went off down by them. As the dust cleared, I could see two bodies lying on the ground, and as I started toward them, they got up, brushed themselves off, and remarked how close it was.

We soon headed out to help our buddies. Billy and Jerry were in front of me, and as I started to go by them to the guys who were yelling for a corpsman, Billy stopped me and checked out the area a little at a time, then motioned me on. The wounded had started back to the rear of the platoon, and Taylor, who had gotten hit in the leg with a 50 caliber, was my first patient. Luckily, his femur wasn't broken, so I bandaged his thigh wound and moved on.

I could hear numerous guys yelling for a corpsman, so I moved on to the nearest one. As I started down the trail, Jerry yelled for me to get down, which I did without hesitation. Then he came to me, telling me we had no one over there. Who was calling then? Unbelievable. It was a gook, and he would later take out his revenge for not getting me. Billy motioned me forward to where a color guy, and another radio man had gotten hit by shrapnel from a chicom, which is their type of hand grenade. As I was patching them up, the gook who had apparently been calling me came up the path I was headed down and threw a chicom at us. I lay over the guy I was treating, so he wouldn't get injured any worse than he was already.

Another guy picked up the chicom and threw it back; however, it blew off in his hand. Frank had got the gook as he rounded the trail and pumped him full of M-16 rounds. Just before the chicom went off, Billy Bradley had jumped on top of me and thus sheltering me with his body. It absorbed the shrapnel that I would have gotten had it not been for him. Thank goodness they weren't serious rounds though. The guy who had attempted to return the chicom to its sender was lying on the ground begging me to kill him. "Just one bullet, Doc. Kill me, Doc. Don't make me suffer any longer." His wounds were serious; however, he was going to make it out of here, and I reassured him of that. He had lost his right hand for the most part; extensive shrapnel in his arms, right leg, and abdomen. Also he had a sucking chest wound, all that trying to save his buddies.

Big Red came over with George Drenth and acted as cover for me. Red, at seeing the guy's hand, said, "Doc, look at his hand." Giving him a searching look, I said that that wasn't so bad and evidently remembering my first aid classes where I stressed to keep calm and not alarm the victim; he said, "Yeah, Doc, you're right. That's not that bad." First, I had to apply a tourniquet to keep the extensive bleeding where his radial artery had been severed. While placing my hand over his chest wound, it was not so tight that it would stop circulation; however, tight enough to stop the profuse bleeding. Next, I stopped his sucking of a chest wound by applying an airtight seal in the chest wound. I made him as comfortable as possible and started human albumin in his good arm because he indeed had lost a considerable amount of blood. Placing him in the shock position, I moved on, leaving George there to protect him. I treated the other guys who had gotten hit also and moved forward.

I continued to run from place to place treating the wounded, which were numerous. As soon as they had said they had found fresh trails, I decided to bring that extra bag of battle dressings just in case. I am sure glad I did. They were bringing Spence down the hill now. He, Angel, and Balue were the first three guys to get hit. Lifer Wright was also up there, but he didn't get hit. Someone was walking with him. He had served his four years in the Air Force and had recently joined the marines, hence the name Lifer

Wright. He had lain on the hill for damn near four hours playing dead a few feet from the machine gun nest which had taken the life of his buddies; however, he was powerless to do anything without losing his life. He lay there until the jets came and then made a dash. He had made it off the hill. Now he wonders why the hell he joined the Marine Corps.

As they pulled Spence past me, I asked what was wrong with him. "He got it in the arm," was Doc Eveland's reply. Catching a 50-slug in the arm wasn't bad compared to some of the other injuries treated already. He had lain on the hill for forty-five minutes before they could get him down, and if it weren't for Outlaw, who ran up the hill with a makeshift stretcher made from the material at hand, bamboo and a poncho, and helped him down, he probably would have been up there a lot longer. He was in a deep state of shock, so I had Eveland finish patching the belly wound I was tending to and decided to give Spence some human albumin. Sure glad that I had some of the guys carry some bottles for me. Upon checking his wound, I noticed that it not only got his arm, but went clean into his chest. I closed the wound, making it airtight and turned him on his injured side to give him the full benefit of his good lung. I started the albumin and prayed that he got out quickly. That was his only chance.

The Marine Corps didn't have very many Hueys, which could whip right in and out. They only had the old Army rejects, the Chinooks, a larger and more cumbersome bird. After finishing, I was off again. I was running out of battle dressings and began improvising more than ever. The arty was coming indirectly on the enemy's positions but never stopped the guns. I was glad that Terry had gone on R&R yesterday because he would have been right up there with Spence and possibly meets the same fate.

I began wondering how my other buddies were making out, and before night fall, I would find out and would proudly shed a tear for all the brave men who didn't make it, especially my good buddy Angel (David Wright). He had been my assistant in the second squad and did a damn good job when I wasn't around, my assistant in first aid class and my close compatriot when reminiscing about our women back home. I told him of Paula who had gotten married just a while before I was heading off to Nam and how that vacuum had been filled by Lynne who I used to date occasionally while in school. I told him how we considered a life together. He in return related about his girl Angel who he loved dearly and was going to marry once he got home. Angel would never get to marry her now because he had caught two fifty rounds in the chest which ended the life. The Lord let him go quickly, something he always mentioned in our talks, and I thanked him for that.

As the fighting continued, I made my way to a small clearing when the jets came in for the strike. I began waving an iridescent flag, so the pilot could see our position, thus avoiding more American casualties. When they called me again, another fellow grabbed the flag, making sure our position was well marked. Before the afternoon was over, he would become one of my patients after getting hit in the leg.

A jet came screaming in, letting its deadly cargo of napalm free. It was so close to our position that it damn near sucked all the air from our lungs when it ignited. I began heading for the CP after the air show was finished. First I saw Lt. Myers talking on the air frequency. I could hear the pilot yelling over the radio that the gooks were running down the side of the hill. The jet nearly hit the ground while pinpointing its target with its bombs. In his next breath, he let us know they weren't running anymore. Lt. Myers told me a few guys were hit up the trail from him a ways. I saw the four men lying there and seeing no one else around, I thought of employing the help of Myers; however, he was too busy with the radios, so I went on alone. After all, if he and Sgt. Chapman kept calling in their accurate air and arty strikes, we would be out in no time.

The first guy I went to rebuffed my plea to find out what was his problem by sounds that were barely audible while he laid there expressionless and gazing off into the distance. I asked if he was hit and where. He mumbled something to the effect that he didn't know, so I quickly checked his body, leaving his helmet and flak jacket on because they were still shooting at us. Finding nothing, I moved on to the next fellow, who was dead already. A fifty round had caught him in the head, ending the life of another machine gunner. He took Richards's place after he had been killed earlier in the battle. Rodriguez was taking out his revenge on his friend's death when he met the same fate.

As I began moving toward the next man, the gooks opened up. I hit the ground as the bullets were splitting it up all around me but never found its mark. The cracking and splitting sound of the bamboo was frightening.

This fellow that I had just reached had gotten grazed in the head, and the bullet lodged in his thigh. I patched him up and dragged him past the higher position and returned to the next man. This was Sack, the colored fellow from Chicago who had given me the beer when I first arrived in country. He too was grazed in the head, and it lodged in his hip. We were a mere fifteen feet from the machine guns nest, which for us had a disadvantageous slope which could cut us down easily if you were doing anything except kissing the ground.

Even if I had a frag, which I no longer carried, I could not reach their position because of the dense canopy overhead. Besides that, their position was too well dug in. Our air strikes did little harm with direct hits, so rest assured a frag would do nothing unless I could get right up there and drop it into their gun opening. I immediately dropped the idea when they began firing again. I, more than anything else, wanted to make it home alive. Putting the dressing on Sack's head, they opened up again, and I could see the gun barrel of their blazing machine gun. How the hell was I going to get out of here was by me. They had such an advantageous position looking right down our throats. I made it once, however, and could do it again. When the firing stopped, I began pulling Sack back toward the rear of the platoon as I had the guy before him. Again, he opened up on us, but we were shielded by a tree that had fallen due to the air strikes.

We stayed behind our shield until the firing stopped and again, we moved on. I was pulling Sack by the back of his flak jacket while he pushed with his good leg. Fortunately, the bullet had only lodged in his hip region and not shattered his pelvis; therefore, he was able to help in his evacuation. I got him back to the position, past the leuy and had one of the other guys bring him back further. His departing words were, "Thanks for not forgetting us, Doc." With this I moved back to my previously held deadly perch and gave the last guy alive up there a good going over. I was greeted by the ghastly sound of the machine gun tearing down the bamboo which surrounded me. Again, I guess that God had come back with me because I had made it back up there alive. Now all I hoped for was to once again make it back down that deadly trail.

There were so many wounded that I hadn't time to take my forty-five out of its protective plastic yet. If I came face-to-face with Charlie, I could be a goner by the time I got my weapon out. By the time I got back to that third man, I was physically exhausted. The running around, the heat, no time for a drink, and the crawling and dragging of bodies, both dead and wounded, had begun to take its toll on me. My heart was pounding in my throat every time that machine gun began playing its deadly melody, and my mouth was as dry as a drought. I promised myself that after I got the guys back, I would rest a few minutes and take a quick drink of water.

Again, I felt his legs while asking him if he hurt any. He assured me he didn't. He told me quite explicitly that he couldn't move, so I checked his back and neck. Nothing. His head was all that was left, so I decided to take off his helmet. Shit. Holy Christ. As I pulled off his helmet, it acted like a suction only to reveal a ghastly side. The back of his skull cap had been blown off and the penetrating hole was covered by part of his skull. The entrance had been hidden by his position on the ground. Part of his brain had been exposed, and the sight was nauseating. I managed to put a light compress on his head which would stop the bleeding but would not cause additional injuries by some part of his shattered skull entering the exposed brain. I called for help, so we could get him back without too much disturbance. No help came, but the gooks opened up on us again.

I lay over his chest to prevent him from getting hit again. When the gooks opened up again, they hit my one and only canteen. Those dirty bastards. I only brought one because I didn't figure we would be here too long. The rest were with my other gear where we had landed. They stopped, and I tried again. We were making a little progress. We had already reached the tree which had fallen that afternoon. Sack and the other fellow were taken over it, but they were able to help me. Perhaps I could get him under that small opening because every other time we were over it, the NVA opened on us. Word was that there were plenty of them out there, which I didn't doubt. Evidently, and unfortunately for us, we had stumbled upon one of their base camps.

Anyway, I rolled over the tree and extended my arm to reach my victim. I couldn't because the space under it just wasn't large enough. I began digging frantically with my hands. Was it large enough now? I was practically underneath it and reached his flak jacket. I had put my cartridge belt under his head to raise it, seeing he was facing downhill, and that was a bad position unless his head could be raised, so we could reduce the pressure of the blood going to his head. Slowly I began to pull him toward me. We were on the other side of the tree now, and just down the bend in the trail I would come across the leuy's new position. When I reached him, Prezarra, who came from Pennsylvania, gave me a hand getting him back a little further. I told them about Rodriguez and the machine gun, and the two guys went back for his body.

Soon thereafter, you could hear the machine gun blaze away. No one yelled for corpsmen, and soon afterward, they returned with Rodriguez' body. We had retrieved all the dead and wounded, and now we were headed out. The first platoon which had been sent to our aid began pulling back to our base camp where we had landed. They too had taken a heavy toll, and as we mustered up our strength to help carry the dead and wounded back, all hell broke loose on the other side of the hill. It wasn't over yet. They said there were a couple of snipers on the other side of the ridge, so we sent out our snipers to get them. These guys who distinguished themselves as marksmen and were equipped with Remington 500s with scopes, the other carried a heavier M1. As they crawled up the hill, everyone was counting on their marksmanship in order that they get their man so we could get out of there. They were followed by a squad from the first platoon.

As they reached the crest of the hill, you could see from our vantage point four gooks, two on each side of them, open up on them before they knew what hit them. Chicoms were thrown at the squad members as they opened up on the assailants. One fell for certain. We had let them outflank us. We were surrounded. We couldn't get any of the medevacs out, and some, without treatment, would surely die during the night. At the moment, I was with the fellow who had his hand blown off. I was hesitant about giving him morphine for pain because I thought he would be back in the rear hospitals in no time. It looks as though I was wrong. To relieve his pain, I finally gave him a surett [sic] of morphine because it appeared that we would be here quite some time. It was damn near dark already. Would this be the end of the first and second platoon of Bravo 1/9? Some thought so, and I was one of them.

We were stranded, had very little ammunition, no food or water, and only a few of our wounded had made it out. The lead was too thick for choppers to land, so we sent our walking wounded ahead. Evidently, they had made it before the gooks had outflanked us. There was no word, however, if they had made it back or not. Among them was Jerry Wright, and now, at least two hours after they had left, there was still no word. We had to count them as MIAs, Missing In Action. Did they too get killed on the way back? I hoped not. Jerry had to get back to his wife and son. Also there were nine other guys with him, and I am quite sure they all had someone home waiting for them. Things were jumpy back at the base camp too. They thought they had movement all around them. Finally, our ten MIAs showed up, but someone on the line heard the movement and, thinking it was the gooks, set off one of the Claymore mines, adding injuries to injuries. They were all medevaced out that night unaware of our fate.

Lt. Tiloan, Lt. Myers, Sgt. Chapman, and Sgt. Letona began organizing the remaining troops. So far, David Wright, Balou (who had paperwork to be completed in the rear and would be leaving as soon as it was done because his brother was over here and, unfortunately, he died before they were completed), Richards, Rodrigo, the two snipers, the fellow that Red carried to me for nearly five hundred yards before hurting his back when he fell, were all dead. Before the day was out, the count would be nine dead. How many of the injured would hold out the night? These men paid the ultimate price anyone could pay for freedom that everyone back home was exercising and needless to say enjoying. How many Americans know the mental anguish we are exposed to? How many appreciate what we are doing? At times I wondered.

Countless others were wounded today, and they would carry their scars forever, which would become a haunting experience for life. They would become "casualties of war" in a different way. For the rest of their lives, they would see those lifeless bodies, bodies of buddies lying in pools of their own blood. Friends screaming in pain will wake them at night. No choppers coming in to take their buddies to the hospital could ever be forgiven. And the fact that we were forewarned about their presence was unforgivable. Yes, the dog trainer was leading his dog up the trail. It sensed danger, and he told Sgt. C. He refused to go further, so Sgt. C moved the men out anyway. Why hadn't he listened to him? We didn't get more than fifty feet before they opened up. Of course if he hadn't called in such accurate arty and air strikes, none of us may have gotten out of it also. For his accuracies, he was awarded a battlefield commission and was up for the Navy Cross. To me it was at the expense of seven men's lives, not to mention the injuries.

Sgt. Letona went around taking a count of the ammunition we had left, which wasn't much and redistributed it as evenly as possible. Garrett and I had one little section which had friendly only on the left and right. Generally, you form a circle like a wagon train used to do. However, we didn't have enough men. We had three hand grenades, one of which Garrett did not claim he had, thus giving us a little more protection, and my .45 with its ten shells. Broken guns were being pieced together to make one workable weapon.

Hearing the wounded moaning, I decided to get all of them together, thus giving less of our positions away. Doc Quinn, a real fine man who would be put up for a bronze star for his heroic actions throughout the day, and I would take care of them throughout the night. I gave my weapon to Garrett and made it to a fairly clear area where we could deal with the men. Everything was silent except the moaning which pierced the night. We administered morphine where needed and hoped for the best. I was given a quick report on the casualties I didn't know and gave a quick one on the ones Quinn didn't know. After I was finished, I told Doc Quinn to see if he could get some sleep, however he gave me first cracks at the hay. I couldn't sleep, but it was nice to just rest for a minute or two.

Doc Stevers came around with McNeely who had been one of the squad members to go with the snipers. He had gotten shot in the arm, but a shrapnel hole in his chest had gone undetected. They called me over. He looked as though he had more than a shot-up arm. Perhaps he had lost a lot of blood on the hill. He definitely was in a severe state of shock. One of the other corpsmen had a bottle of Ringers lactate left, so I started it on him. Then I started to check him over thoroughly, coming across the shrapnel hole. Perhaps it had nicked a vein or artery. At any rate, he had lost a considerable amount of blood, and before I was done examining him, his breathing and circulation ceased. I started closed cardiac massage while Doc Quinn joined in with mouth-to-mouth resuscitation. We worked well over an hour, but it was to no avail. McNeely had died. He now made the eight.

After we placed Mack with the dead, we checked the others, and we started to give the guy who had the back of his head blown off morphine. He was moaning continuously, and as a rule, a head injury should never get morphine. We decided to give it to him, however, because it would calm him down some. It worked. Now all we hoped for was that he would make it through the night. Spence was bad off also, and we knew if he held out to morning, he would have a good chance. The water was completely exhausted by this time, and as the wounded pleaded for some, all we could do was give them something to chew on to get their saliva glands excreting. I myself was chewing the filter of a Salem. To me it was refreshing.

As I was going to wake Jim, word was passed to keep as low as possible and light a heat tap in front of your position. They could see the silhouettes of the gooks on an adjoining hill. They thought the attack was near. I prayed to God to let me die quickly. I knew the end was at hand, and all I wanted now was to go as quickly as possible. The heat tap would mark our positions while the jets gave us support when the time came.

Spence had failed on us, and there was nothing we could do for him, and God knows how hard we tried. He was the ninth man to die today, and as Jim told me to lay down for a while, I prayed for these great men, most of them are friends of mine who had given their lives for what at times seem to be useless; a corrupt government that was bleeding Uncle Sam of its young potential, as well as its funds. Who knows, one of the guys who have so far died over here could have someday found the cure for cancer, maybe be the president or perhaps even instrumental in helping world peace. Now we will never know.

Everything appeared to be quiet when someone opened up in the line. Everyone tensed up waiting for wave after wave of gooks coming to storm our poorly equipped positions. I could remember reading a story once about some army sergeant who was in a similar predicament and ended up fighting the enemy hand by hand. Would this be our grand finale? Soon it would be the break of dawn, and then they would attack. My plea again echoed throughout my mind. Please, Lord, make me go quickly. Make me go quickly.

Dawn was here, yet they hadn't attacked. Why? We could see their silhouettes moving on the hills during the night. Were they waiting for us on the trail? Setting up another ambush? Air strikes were called in as day broke. Rounds impacted all around our outer perimeter. Indeed, the sergeant was calling in the arty right on the nose. From our base camp, another platoon was heading out to cover for us as we pulled back. We could see Big Brother in the air. Suddenly it scoped down on our relief column thinking they were gooks. Many more of our men were injured, and I would find my buddy Richards, who was company radio man, had lost an eye.

The CO and gunny would be heading back to the states because of their injuries. Will there be no end to their needless suffering? After the air strikes, we called an arty to lay a smoke screen which would allow us to carry the dead and wounded over the hill rather than around the side which supported a sixty degree decline. The smoke screen was laid on the wrong side of the hill. Correction after correction made it worse. Rather than risk the chance of getting mortared while across the hill, we took the more precarious way around the side. The first squad began making their way along the side of the mortar hill. Footing was lost constantly, and they had all they could do to prevent the body from rolling down the steep embankment into the ravine below.

After they got a ways out, the second-to-last group, of which I was a part, began moving out. Every once in a while a mortar would go off, but we kept up the pace. We had found two of their dead on the hill. They must be the ones who got hit after getting our snipers. I crawled up and took a canteen of water from the body and passed it on to the wounded. I was in the rear of the platoon in order to treat anyone who may get hit while we were pulling back. Most of our wounded had already made it across, and there was one more body behind us. Again, someone lost their footing. I lay in front of the poncho which we were carrying the dead in to prevent it from going down the hill any further. My mental awareness was all but functioning when Dave's face rolled out of the poncho and faced me. One out of nine chances and I had to carry Dave's.

My eyes reddened as tears began to flow. The mortars were raining in on us now. We were ordered to leave the bodies and make a run for it. Not Dave's. I hear what they do to the bodies once they were left out. They weren't going to cut off his testicles and stuff them in his mouth. They weren't going to cut off his head and cram it in his belly. They weren't going to hang him from a tree or place a booby trap under his body. They weren't going to mutilate my friend, not if I could help it anyway. Everyone had left the bodies when word was passed to head for home. I tried to drag Dave by myself. I tried and tried until someone grabbed my arm and said, "Come on, Doc. They are dead. No sense adding to the toll." Finally the word "survival" lit up, and I was off running down the trail like the others to our base camp. The mortars were following us all the way. We managed to stay one step ahead of them. They were dropped to light the pathway.

About thirty-five hours after our little patrol went out to check the area, we were back. It was a tragic toll and for what? Forty-six men went out with us unharmed, and only nineteen returned in the same manner. The other platoon also lost about half of their men to injuries. Nine deaths totaled so far. Many may still die from their wounds. I ask you, for what?

We'll leave here soon. The Ghost Battalion and the Walking Dead became synonymous with Bravo 1/9. This has happened before and will undoubtedly happen again. We'll go somewhere, hit the shit, and leave a few days later. Is there any meaning to this madness? When we reached our base camp, that colored fellow was there to greet me and hand over his canteen to me. I made it to the foxhole we had dug the morning we arrived there and all but collapsed from exhaustion. Bradley was soon by my side, and I passed the water on to him. A chopper was inbound with an external [sic] of water, so we had plenty now. Last night and this morning, I would have been satisfied with a taste.

Anyway, all the wounded were to be on the LZ and ready to leave on the inbound bird. Bill was hesitant about going, thinking his injury wasn't bad enough. You just get your ass on that chopper and get the hell out of here. It didn't make much convincing, and Bill was off.

When the chopper approached, we could see it had no water. It had deposited it at another area. Thanks a lot guys. As it began to land, all hell broke loose. The chopper was blazing away with its fifties, and the occupants were standing at the window, firing at a couple of snipers who kept us at bay all the next day.

Barney, who had been on R&R, had chosen a hell after time to come back. He brought with him a new man, Paul Manerol. He didn't figure in as the marine type, more of the mothering boy type. He too would lose his life over here and again, I ask for what? We had just lost nine men while being bait for the South Vietnamese government, exposing their foes. After all, none of us have enemies in Hanoi. If we were so worried about stopping communism, why not start at home. Why are we fighting?

I once thought I knew when I saw those prisoners when I first got in country, but now I don't know. These people are human beings just as we are and evidently are fighting for something they believe in because they fight hard and proud. This is something you can't take away from them. Wave after wave was attacking a fire support base. The first wave jumped on the barbed wire while repeated waves ran over them. After the battle, kids who are fifteen at the most were found dead. When I first got here, everyone called them gooks, then it was Charlie, and now it was Charles. They go against our jet planes, our big guns, our tanks, and our superior forces. Indeed at times he deserved more respect than he got.

As night fell, we took up the positions we had dug when we landed two days ago. Tonight, we would fight a battle, but it would be of a different nature. Psychological. Evidently, the main body of NVA troops had withdrawn to escape further air attacks and arty; however, they left a few men to play with our minds. Claymore mines and trip flares were set up only to be tampered with by Charlie. Somehow in the dark they found them, turning the claymores toward our positions, and the trip wires were cut without tripping the flares. Our perimeter defense was gone, unaware to us at the moment.

Around midnight, we got movement. Soon thereafter, Charlie was out there saying "Nine marines die. Nine marines die." One of the guys on the line couldn't bear it any longer, and knowing his claymore mine was in the vicinity of the voice, he marked his hell box, thus detonating it, only to have it shower our troops. Most guys were down, and no serious injuries were sustained. Word was passed about the mines. Frags were thrown to silence the enemy but to no avail. Two more hours they kept our nerves on edge. Have they done anything to the bodies? After all, they have the right count. I hope not. God, they wouldn't, would they?

They were talking about our buddies who we had to leave out there. Doc Zimmerman was on a mission once where they had to retrieve the bodies of quite a few Americans who were killed. When they got back to the battle area, their heads were in their stomachs, their balls in their mouth. Of course they weren't the only barbaric ones. One corpsman was sent to the rear after he chopped off the head of a dead gook, others were known to collect their ears and dropping POWs from choppers was heard of.

After two hours of making us psychological casualties, there was a flurry of movement about the lines. Were they getting ready for a full-scale attack? Sgt. C was making rounds of the line to make sure everyone was up. Little did he realize no one could sleep on a night like this. When he got to our hole (there was no moon, clouds were in the sky, and it presented a dark arena), Frank yelled, "Halt." The sergeant was so startled that he could barely tell us who he was. He finally sensed the tenseness of the troops and decided it would be beneficial for his health to return to his position and stay there, which he did without second thought.

As dawn came around, a platoon was sent from Delta Company to help us out. We had lost over a platoon of men already, so we weren't up to full strength yet. Word was passed to get ready because we were going back out not to get our guys as previously planned, but we were going to take those machine guns. Morale was at its lowest peak I had ever seen. The men from mortars hadn't given went out with us at first, and now they were fighting among themselves. Bittner came up to me and said, "Doc, you got to get me out of here." Here is a man who has done his time and had only ten days left before his rotation date, and they wanted him to go back out on a suicide mission. Bullshit. If there was anything I could do, it would be done. "Let me see that finger, trigger finger, isn't it? "As I smashed down on it, he began to say "yes." When my hand hit his finger, instead he let out a yell. I didn't break it, but it was dislocated. I medevaced him to the next bird without anyone knowing until he had left.

At the other end of the platoon, a shot went off. "Corpsman" rang out loud and clear. Was it an AD or a self-inflicted wound? "Gee, Doc, I was cleaning my gun, and it went off. Thought I had all the rounds out of the chamber. Good thing I had it pointed downward. Would have been hell catching it in the chest." The foot is bad enough. He just caught the little toe, which was gone. No one deserves to die on a mission such as the one they have planned out for us, and some guys were willing to go to great extents to make sure they wouldn't go. Was he one? He knows and will have to live with it the rest of his life. Another "casualty of war."

They told us we would be going down in the valley and sneak up behind him as if we were going to yell "surprise" and capture the lot of them. Only

John Wayne can do that, and that's only in the movies. Are they stupid or crazy? There must be an answer somewhere. It was 2:00 in the afternoon already, and it was I believe possible to get down there to take the hill before dark. Besides, all that water never came, and we only had one canteen a piece, which would not last long in this heat. Food was down; medical supplies were what we were able to sponge from the other corpsmen who didn't go out with us.

I returned with only five dressings when I went out there with nearly one hundred. We had nothing, yet the damn Marine Corps insisted that we proceed with untiring determination and steadfast devotion. Fuck them. They must be crazy. If they wanted to get those damn guns which direct hit from jets couldn't silence, let them but not at my expense or that of my buddies.' Sure they were in the rear. They had no worries. We were the ones to face the lead. If we had just one heat casualty while trying to get through that thick underbrush, we were done for it. We only had six guys left in our squad, and if one, just one, succumbed to the extensive heat, you must remember the sparse water supply, the fatigue of the proceeding two days, we would be in a bind. It would take four men to carry him, and the last guy would be carrying his gear. The other squads were in the same predicament.

They had sent a colonel out to direct the operation from here, and I decided to talk to him. I requested Mast and was going to explain our beef. I could do it without fear of repercussions because I wasn't a marine. I could always say my attitude was from a medical standpoint. Of course that wasn't true. Actually, I was tired of seeing that needless bloodshed which would give some lifer in the rear the Distinguished Service medal, a noncom in the field a commission, officers put up for Navy Crosses and so forth, all at our expense.

Finally, three squad leaders decided to go with me. We went through the chain of command and finally got to our leuy. We realized that it would be to no avail, but we had to try at least to let ourselves know that we had exhausted all avenues. It was quite evident all around them that we weren't willing to go. We got as far as the major. Bravo Company, put up for the Navy Cross because of the twenty-second, explained our view for us, looks as though we were going out anyway. At least we satisfied ourselves knowing we tried everything. How could they actually believe that we could take their positions now, unless they had pulled out? And if they did, what good and merit would our toils bring? Would we be stranded out there again tonight with the gooks all around us, or would we be dead by tonight? Why play games with our lives?

Soon they told us to stagger our packs. We weren't going back out to take their positions; we were going back for our dead. Did we have any part in changing their minds? Probably not. But we weren't going back to "Slaughter Ridge." A new fear took hold as we left the perimeter. What have they done to the bodies? It was now 3:30, and soon we would find out.

"D" companies lead the way, setting up men on the trail to act as security, so we wouldn't get ambushed again. We advanced through them as we proceeded on to Mortar Hill where the bodies were lying. After about half an hour, an M-79 (grenade launcher) round went off. Everyone hit the dirt and wondered if this was the beginning of another ambush. Soon, word filtered back that it was an AD (accidental discharge.) One of the guys carrying a body tripped in the thick underbrush, and his weapon went off, catching him in the face. As we advanced, we see his buddies leading him back to the base camp. His whole face was bandaged.

Word was passed back that the gooks hadn't touched any of the bodies; however, nature and her elements had began taking their course. The bodies were bloated and were beginning to decompose due to the heat. Two days in the sun had deprived the parents of an open-casket funeral. It was a ghastly sight. No one could ever forget those bodies. A tear may be shed twenty years from now when a flashback occurs, hate and discontent may follow, questions left unanswered may remain that way, some may pass it off, others may not be able to for a while. Nonetheless, we will all be casualties, mental casualties for the rest of our lives.

The bodies were unrecognizable; however, I was afraid I would get Angel's body again, so I carried the weapons. I couldn't bear seeing him in his present state. The ponchos were ripping. Branches were tearing into the bodies. Vomitous on the side of the trails. How long could these guys hold out? This indeed was a mental strain. Smitty had flipped out already. Would there be more? Up ahead a guy fell and strained his back muscles while trying to keep the body from hitting the ground when he tripped. Now we needed two guys to help him.

It was getting dark, and they called in a flare ship to illuminate the sky, so we could make it in tonight. The going was rough to say the least. Reaching the perimeter, I told a leuy to send some men out with a couple of ponchos and help get the last two bodies in. We did as I made it to our CP. They wanted me to check the guy on the LZ (the one who was hit in the face). Bob went out to help with the other guy they were bringing in with the back strain.

On the LZ, I saw Doc Provance who had come a day after I arrived. I had to make sure that that fellow made it on the bird which was inbound. I redressed his injury, making it more comfortable. One eye was still good. His nose would need a lot of surgery to improve its appearance. Otherwise, he had a ticket home.

Doc Wecker finally arrived with our back victim, and the bird was approaching. I recruited a few guys to load the bodies aboard. Still were two more out there on their way in. I had just strapped the guy in when a sniper opened up on the chopper. He took off taking Wecker with them and leaving two of the dead behind, excluding the two still on the trail.

After the last two bodies had reached the perimeter, we set up our watch. It was dark now, and the flare ship had left. We were on our own again. If we could only make it through the night, tomorrow we were leaving. At least that's the word. While on watch, we had two from each hole at a time. Fear and imagination took over. Who was that? Halt. Who was there? Morning came around, and we were all anxious to leave our hell on earth. Big guns went off within the DMZ.

Soon word came over the radio that Delta Company was taking incoming. We got bearing and sent in our grid coordinates. Two secondary explosions were recorded, so we must have made a few direct hits. Before leaving, however, we had to clean the area. Keep Vietnam clean. Pick up your area before you leave. Nothing was left that they could use, and the trash was burned. Extra C-rats were punctured and buried. At one point, a frag went off in a foxhole. Someone burning their trash hadn't seen the frag. Luckily, it hadn't caused any injuries. After the explosion, one guy laid on the ground, saying nothing and not moving. Evidently, the rigors of the past few days had finally come to a head after the explosion which was so close to him. He didn't say a word the rest of the day and was helped aboard the first chopper, and all to see him were greeted with a vacant stare, a definite case of battle fatigue.

When were we getting out? When there are some choppers available was the reply. Damn ill-equipped Marine Corps. This wasn't the first time we had to wait and wait. Rest assured, it wouldn't be the last. The word was that they were going to do away with the Marine Corps and thus to many destroy a bit of American heritage. To combat this, the Marine Corps returns part of its budget each year, showing how they can still function on such a menial fee. Of course, if they used that extra money for more and better equipment, maybe Spence and McNeely would have made it out the other day and perhaps be alive today. The Marine Corps was fighting for its survival, but again, at our expense.

About three o'clock, the choppers began arriving. They had been out on a resupply mission. Now it was our turn to leave. Delta's platoon was first to leave. I was to be on the first chopper of the next wave. As I ran past the pilot, I gave him the thumbs-up sign. We indeed were thankful to them. We were leaving this hell-hole. Before I was able to board, a mortar round went off fifty feet away, and the bird was off with a few guys who had managed to get on. Upon impact, everyone hit the ground. I made a flying leap and landed in a foxhole atop Sgt. Letona.

As the next chopper approached, I was going to make certain I got aboard. As soon as it was settling, I ran toward it along with many other guys. The noise of the rotor blades obliterated the sounds from the mortar tubes. The rounds began to fall again, and the chopper took off. I lunged forward and just managed to get a hold of one of the legs to the seat. Holding on for dear life, we leaped into the air. I felt something clawing at my leg. Glancing around, I saw someone slipping out the door, which I had barely made it to. Quickly I grabbed his pack and yelled for help. The door was closing up, and if I could hold on just a little longer, we would make it. The tail gunner and others began dragging the man in. The body rolled over and looked at my filing and said, "Thanks, Doc." It was Andy.

Once airborne, I thanked God for getting us out of there and prayed that the rest of the guys be just as lucky. Upon landing at Stud, we waited for the rest of the men of Bravo 1/9 on the LZ before we took it easy. We had to be sure that our buddies, what remained of them, made it back okay. Each chopper was greeted cordially. They let us know that the rounds landed right on the LZ after our bird took off. Three guys trying to get on were wounded. It's a damn good thing that Arnold and I didn't fall out.

Next day, we would find out that numerous guys would be put up for decorations. Services would be held for our comrades who didn't make it. Many guys would be headed home because of the extent of their injuries, and others, unfortunately, would return to the unit once they had recuperated from their wounds in the rear.

We ate well that night and had a few beers and had a wonderfully peaceful night at Stud. When morning came around, we took showers and cleaned our clothes. Also, we were told to stand by. Someone was catching the shit behind the Rock Pile, and we were going in to help. Hell, we didn't even have a day off to recuperate. Again, we were racing headlong into battle. What do they think we are?

Before we left, however, we were commended on what a fine job we did by some silly colonel who noted the progress behind some desk in the rear. To him, the best thing in the world was the body count. Eliminate those gooks. We paid dearly, however, but did he realize just how dearly it was? He kept telling us we were responsible for rendering a gook regiment ineffective. Also indirectly, we were responsible for the death of well, over a thousand NVA. Believe it or not, to be more accurate, he told us the number was two thousand five hundred/. I've seen two. I just wonder how much of this shit they tell us and the American people are true.

August 28. We were boarding choppers again and heading for a valley which is seeing distance from the Rock Pile. As we landed, we could see rockets being launched from the hill to our right. We fanned out and were ready for anything as the rest of the choppers landed. They cut us a hut and let us defend the big CP. As we were placed in temporary positions, the 106s were putting themselves into position. We had never been on an OP before where they were used, and when we see a colonel's aid carrying a shitter made from an ammo box, that took the cake. In a war zone, our brass saw it fit to have a man carrying his shitter. Was he too damn good to squat or use a cat hole? Evidently so. Wonder if he has someone to wipe his ass too?

It was getting dark, and we still weren't in position for that night. Our efficient Marine Corps moved us around like checkers, as usual. This happens every time we sit in, but it still gets to you after a while. Okay. Dig in. This is where we'll be.

Fifteen minutes later. Come on, let's go if you want to get set in before dark. Finally, it ended up that night sleeping on a slope bracing yourself against a bush, tree, or anything available which would prevent you from rolling down the hill. Tension still ran high among the troops, and this shuttling around didn't help much.

When morning came around, we moved out, again taking up positions on the side of another hill. We would run patrols out of here every day for the next week. Hopefully then, we'll go in for a while. The patrols lasted damn near all day and covered a lot of rugged terrain. It wasn't bad here, however, seeing we got enough food and water, and there wasn't any action because other units were all around us. It pays to stick with the big CP because we too reaped their bennies. It was so safe here that General Davis came out to pay us a visit. He really thought a lot of his men and even once used his chopper to bring us the mail. I would get to see a lot of him once I get out of the bush.

They had B-52ed the area before we went into it, and it was now our job to check it out. Across the valley we had landed in. Charlie Company was engaged in a firefight with the enemy. Air strikes were called in, and we could see the battle in progress. They soon called our platoon together, and we were headed out on an all-day patrol. When we reached the battled-scared area of the B-52 strikes, we were aghast at the destruction they can do. I was thankful that I wasn't a gook. Imagine what they could do to you. I was in back of a gigantic rock unearthed by the fury of the explosions and remained there until they had checked out the area. Our lead element thought they heard someone. Outlaw thought he had actually seen a hand on a tree. Could it be true, or were we still jumpy from last week? Rest assured we were very cautious.

After the search was completed with negative results, we continued, carefully contemplating another ambush. About fifty yards up the trail, our lead man got down again. A squad went up either side of the trail about ten yards off on each side while we remained at the trail entrance watching. Even Sgt. C was as grungy [sic] as he was, didn't want a repeat of last week. After the men reached what appeared to be a bunker, we moved forward. Nothing.

The next day and another platoon went out on a patrol while we manned the lines and rested. Mail had arrived, and Lynne hadn't failed me yet, though her letters weren't real regular anymore. I couldn't wait to get home to her. She has really made it a lot easier for me over here. I knew we would make a wonderful couple with a couple of lovely children running around. Also, I got a letter from my best buddy, Joe McCormick, who mentioned that I had better hurry home, so I could be godfather to his newborn son. I could hardly wait. He had gotten married soon after I left for the Nam. I had met Sue many times before and knew that Joe had lucked out getting such a lovely wife. With Lynne, I would fair out just as well. My main ambition in life was to raise a lovely little family and support them comfortably, and I believe once I got out of the service, I would accomplish it. I couldn't wait until I could fulfill those dreams.

Getting letters while in the bush is probably the most important factor which keeps morale high. I was definitely thankful because I got more than my share. My mom alone wrote three times a week. I had occasional letters from friends, Jackie, and Jimmie, and Jenny, not to mention the most important to me at the moment, Lynne's. Jenny Berg, who came from Zumbrota, Minnesota, is one of those rare sorts of girls who are simply wonderful. I had met her nearly two years ago in Chicago while I was attending hospital corps school in Great Lakes, Illinois. I had taken her to a show and a walk that weekend, and ever since then we have remained the best of friends. Even now, she sends me packages and cards for every occasion and a letter at least once a week, all which radiate her kind and pleasant personality. She was indeed a girl to love in a different sort of way, the love of a true friendship. Hopefully someday, I would get to see her again.

The patrol that went out met no opposition, and as night fell, everyone remained fairly close to their foxhole in case of any eventuality. At about three in the morning, all hell broke loose down by the 106's. Dr. Dick, who was our battalion surgeon, was on hand and replied to the call. Our men ended up on one of our own men. The man died despite the doctor's valiant efforts to save his life.

When morning came around, we heard that the guy had been wiped out intentionally. This is something that happens every once in a while. (We had one of our platoon members stab another after he stole water.) Officers who didn't give a shit about the men's welfare but were only looking for that promotion and medals were often the targets.

Here, a soldier could kill under the protection of war. I wonder how many of our men died this way. Every time an incident such as this arises, an investigation is begun to determine if it was justifiable or not. How could it be proved otherwise? After testimony was taken from all those involved, it appeared that this fellow went in front of the lines to take a leak. When he returned, he was challenged by the man from the next position. (He had failed to inform anyone where he was going.) He didn't reply, so the line opened up. Perhaps this one was justifiable, but many more weren't.

Our infamous Captain Williams, who clearly was interested in his future as a career officer rather than the life of his men, almost met the same fate. There was a bounty on his head for $7,000. (How it was to be paid was anyone's guess.) The money was supposedly donated to the cause in various denominations not to kill him but just to get him out of the bush. The gooks wounded him before any drastic actions were taken.

At one time, he had sent an ambush through an ambush which was set up already. Needless to say, each thought the other were the enemy. The firefight followed. Soon after the initial firing began, they were yelling commands to squad members, and each finally realized who the other was. However, it wasn't until one guy had lost his life. His best friend walked up to Captain Williams's position with two frags, pins pulled, and one in each hand. He was going to kill Williams even if it meant taking his own life too. Fortunately, he was stopped before he had taken such a drastic measure. Three days later, Williams was medevaced after a gook's mortar round hit near his position. Fortunate for him it had ended that way. Who knows, within a week someone might have tried for that $7,000.

The next day, we went on a patrol again which took us deep into the jungles and mountains. It started out easy enough but soon became unmanageable. As we made our way through the dense foliage, we encountered a 1,000-pound bomb. Man, was I ever glad that I wasn't a gook. Could you imagine being near something as big as that when it went off? Besides that, the U.S. has its jets which always come to the aid of troops who were in trouble. Without Big Brother, we would definitely lose a hell of a lot more guys than we are now.

Anyway, we passed it by and proceeded on. Once over the hill, we took five while contemplating the easiest way to travel. It was so thick that we would never make it back by dark. We proceeded on hacking our way through the dense jungle growth. We soon came to a gully which had been made by the torrential monsoon rains. We decided to follow it down, and before we knew it, it was about four feet deep. Trails went off to the left and right and it was an ideal place for an ambush. The gully turned into a cool, refreshing stream fed by a spring. Indeed, this was a perfect place to camp, and with Slaughter Ridge still in mind, we proceeded very carefully.

At one point, we thought we had movement. We got down and waited. Outlaw checked the area out and finding nothing, came to inform Sgt. Letona. Upon seeing Outlaw round the bend in the stream, the sergeant yelled "Don't shoot. We are Americans." When Outlaw rounded the bend, Maneral [sic] took off his safety. Guess it just showed that everyone was still tense and nervous on edge since the ambush. We decided to spread out more, but we had to go down the stream bed in order to make it in by dark.

After what seemed to be an endless trail, we reached a river and followed the banks for a mile or two where we came to the valley we had landed in. We continued up a hill. And after passing through another valley and climbing its ridge, we would be home. The LP (listening post) was already out as we entered our perimeter exhausted. We settled down to our C-rats, and then I went fast asleep until my time was for watch. It was nice out, so I slept on the ground by the watch rather than in our little shelter, whose main purpose was to protect us from the sun rays. I was looking like a soul brother already with the tan I had. As with the other nights, it went by peacefully.

When morning came, they told my squad we were going on an LP over on the next ridge. It didn't have many trees, and the elephant grass was about five feet tall. There we would have a commanding look over three valleys. Napalm was dropped earlier on one of the far ridges, and the grass was still burning up the side of the mountain. With a change of wind, we would have to prepare ourselves for a firefighting session.

When night came, we moved down into the saddle and set up our night position. Here we would be able to detect any movement on our side of the big CP. If the gooks ever did come, they would have us before we ever had a chance to get back to the perimeter. The night passed uneventfully, and with daybreak, our replacements arrived, and we headed in. They were building a fire support base about a click from us, and as we saw a chopper bringing in a bulldozer, we wondered what was becoming of the Marine Corps, the new action corps stealing the Army's image. Any other time they would make you dig manually. Who knows, perhaps after fifty years, they were beginning to make some progress after all.

After the big guns were in place, we pulled out moving up the valley past the new fire support base. It became infamous like Leather Neck Square, the Razor Beach, and the [can't read] up toward Dong Ha mountain. This was a place to stay away from at the moment, but it looked as though we were headed for trouble again. It became more evident that we were when the big CP was choppered out.

I guessed we moved a few clicks right up the valley bed after the CPs were flown out, and as our luck would have it, the rains began. The river was swelling at a dangerously quick pace, and we knew damn well that once we got across, we would be stranded there unless the rains stopped soon, which didn't look too promising. Mud was already six inches deep as we marched on. We had crossed the river with considerable difficulty, and now it was the third platoon's turn to venture across. They weren't as lucky as we, and the swift current caught their footing and swept them downstream. No one drowned, but six of the guys had to rid themselves of their gear in order to reach the bank. Eager hands were waiting to pull them out.

We bivouacked in an area which was sheltered on three sides by a steep ridge and the river in front of us. It was true that the ridge sheltered us from any gooks from seeing us, but what if they stumbled on us? It was the perfect place to set up a mortar and wipe us out. Lucky for us, we weren't bothered. We stayed there for five days without any supplies, but plenty of water. Our foxholes filled up as soon as they were dug. For the next five days, we couldn't enjoy one minute of the comforts of warmth or dry clothes. We huddled four to a tent made from our ponchos, but the trenches dug around the tent were soon filled with dirt being washed from the ridges, thus making a steady stream of water meandering through our so-called shelter. Stripping down, I stepped outside letting the rain wash some of the crud of Vietnam off my body.

Patrols were also set up, and it was our turn to venture up the mud-slick slopes searching the area for any sign of movement. It became a real chore making your way up the hillside, which was nothing but mud and became worse every time someone slipped. Every step forward soon brought you two steps back. Terry was in front of me, and as he began to fall, I stopped him, only to fall myself. As I got up, I began digging the mud out of my ear.

We made it up the side of the hill and began climbing the ridge to its high point when Red slipped and traveled at least a quarter of a mile down before he stopped himself by grabbing some bush which was at hand. Red yelled he was okay, but his damn helmet went all the way down landing close to the lines. He retrieved it and waited for us to return from the patrol.

Upon reaching the top of the ridge which ran parallel to the river, we came across some American gear and parts of a skeleton femur, parts of the skull, and part of the shoulder blade. It had been there quite some time, and we wondered if it was that of an American soldier who had died so far away from home. When someone found a dog tag, we picked up the remains and brought them back to our pause. Perhaps this would relieve the grief of his parents who were only informed that he was missing in action and presumed dead. Though it couldn't be proven whose remains they were, there was a good chance they were his. Deep down, his parents could believe he was resting in peace.

We reentered our perimeter and settled back down in our shelter. We would soon have a health problem if the rain didn't stop. My feet and hands, no matter how much I tried to keep them dry, were beginning to become an immersion problem. My socks were placed in my shirt to have my body heat keep them dry, but my clothing was so wet it was to no avail. Everyone was complaining from the brass on down. Immersion foot and FUO (fevers of undetermined origin), soon we would need some medevac chopper.

All the supplies were exhausted. Frank Van Noy Hues, a competent foot doctor in his own mind, was suffering from severe immersion foot. The skin was splitting into wide crevices and was susceptible to infection. I gave him the remaining of my foot powder and ordered him to stay off his feet and keep them as dry as possible. It did no good. Damn guy is just plain ignorant. FUO began getting out of hand. One hundred four degrees was the highest so far, and aspirin was given to help bring it down while we let the rain cool him. We maintain it as it was, but soon, very soon he had to get out.

On the first day that the sky began to clear, they let us know that a bird was inbound. We moved back about a half a mile, still on our side of the river and found a good LZ. I help Frank over, along with Flagg, who had a temperature of one hundred three. Paul Manerol, whose hand had a deep-rooted infection, and a few guys from the second squad were brought to the senior corpsman. If there was room, they were to get on the first bird. Before the bird came in, we had thirty-seven medevacs. The chopper never arrived until about five that night. With it came heat taps and C-rats which let us know we would be here for a while. Those to be medevaced left on the bird, all but one that is. As they took off, we dug into our consolation prize and ate well that night. When morning came, they told us to pack up, we were moving out. We again moved toward Dong Ha Mountain. Evidently, it was still our objective.

As we proceeded, we crossed and recrossed the river which had gone down since the rain had stopped. In the distance, we could see a waterfall which appeared to fall nearly a thousand feet straight down. It was so beautiful and peaceful that you could never expect to see it while fighting a war. We sat in just before dark on the riverbank, and as morning came, it proved the ideal place to swim and wash your clothes.

The next day, we searched the immediate area and found that this had once been used by the enemy as a base camp. As long as they weren't in the area now, I didn't mind. Resupplies came in with special treats for all of us such as gallons of peaches, something we had never experienced in the bush before. Along with it came bread, luncheon meat, and catsup which definitely was a treat compared to our accustomed C-rats. I can't say much for luncheon meat with catsup sandwiches, but it sure was a change.

When morning came, we went out on another patrol which followed the stream. This proved to be an escape from the sweltering heat which we now had to contend with seeing the rain had ended. It seems as though we can never find a happy medium weather-wise, but we managed to cope with and adapt to such adverse weather conditions. What else could you do? The scout dog was with Doc Quinn's patrol and had run into two gooks, but they were scared more than us, and they managed to allude us.

As for ourselves, we ran across a few recently traveled trails and found one that was capable of accommodating trucks while keeping it hidden with its jungle canopy. Directional signs were carved into trees along the route which was now damaged by the arc lights (B-52 raids).

On the way back to our base camp, we came across a hutch built at the base of two trees. It was well camouflaged, and we never noticed it until we were right up on it. It had been used recently, perhaps even as short a time ago as this morning. Rice was left on the fire, which by now were only cold embers which led you to believe that they made a hasty retreat.

We got back to our base camp and went swimming. When night came, they put an LP in front of us about fifty feet, so we decided to take advantage of it and sleep the night through. About 11:00 at night, all were awaken when flares went off, leading us to believe that someone had movement on the lines. Everyone was up, holding their breath and listening. Nothing.

In the distance we could hear the faint wail of a chopper, and finally word filtered back that it was an emergency medevac. The only fellow who didn't make it out the day the rains stopped was now fighting a temperature of one hundred six. Probably malaria. It takes its toll over here, and our company had more than its share.

The next day, we were pulled back past Starvation Mountain, as we now called it, and into the area, we were to pull out of about a week ago. They again said we were going in, but we had our doubts. Along with me, I carried the most prized possession of our platoon, a gallon can of peaches. On the way, part of the squad had gotten lost after taking a wrong turn. I told our lead element to stop, which they did reluctantly but only for a short time. Sure we were out in the open now, but there were still guys in the dense foliage.

Once we got off the riverbank, the going was relatively easy; however, we still had plenty of guys behind us who were fighting to keep up while climbing the rocks in the river. Only after we succeeded to lose a squad did our lead element decide to stop. If the area had been infested with gooks, I definitely wouldn't have wanted to be with them. Sure enough though, after we got to our previous LZ, the birds were on their way. We were finally going in. While waiting, we had a feast on the peaches and laid back and relaxed, thinking that we would be resting at LZ Stud for a while at least before we go out again.

The birds brought us back to Stud where we had two cold beers, two cold sodas, a hot meal, and a shower waiting for us. When we woke the next morning, however, we were packing, going to the Rock Pile. We wouldn't be at OP Ben like the last time we were there, but we hoped we would stay a while. We loaded six-bys, and we're on our way. They fanned out around their LZ when we got there, the same one I had departed on the morning of June 18. I didn't know what it held for me then and didn't know now.

Getting to our bunker, we decided to clean it up before we stepped into it. The AVRNS had just left, and the place was in shambles. Garbage was everywhere, and they had failed to use piss tubes and latrines, leaving the area susceptible to every disease imaginable. We all pitched in, thus making our area livable. While cleaning, we were confronted first with a 7-inch centipede. Minutes later, we found a gigantic scorpion. With this, bets were taken to see which one would win. I had the scorpion, as did almost everyone else. It looked like a cockfight with everyone cheering on their pick. Someone dumped our bug juice in with them, followed by a match, and as it went up in flames, the excitement grew. It was cruel, but so is war.

After breaking our ass for a few hours, we had a halfway respectable place to live. Come tomorrow, we would have to try and keep the rain out. But we found out tomorrow we were pulling out. Word was that we were going into the DMZ, something no one looked forward to. Since the Pueblo incident, we had lost some trust in Uncle Sam. What if we were stranded there, especially now seeing that they had halted the bombing, would they come to our aid or let us fend for ourselves? It's all a big political game, and we were the pawns. Power of the gretgo [sic]. Anyway, word was passed to pack up and be ready to leave. We had our gear staged all ready to leave and could see our reliefs getting off the choppers. They would be taking our places as we ventured through one of the enemy's many sanctuaries.

As they approached, we were finishing off a game of Back Alley on top of our bunker when the NVA welcoming committee warned them of their presence. They were greeted with three mortar rounds sent COD from the enemy position. Some were near the Rock Pile itself. Everyone jumped into the closest trench or hole available, and as I was making my way off the bunker, the second of the three detonated with me, watching a piece of shrapnel in the palm of my hand. At first I hadn't noticed it except for an unusual stinging in my hand, but after the welcome ceased, someone began calling for a corpsman. I didn't realize that they were calling him for me. When I got up seeing the blood, I began to feel the pain.

With the sound of "corpsman" still singing out, I thought that someone else was injured and grabbed my bag. It was then that I realized that everyone else was okay. They wanted him for me. I informed them that I was the doc and Heart, who had recently joined us, patched up my hand. Heart was from Arkansas and had to leave behind a wife and lovely little daughter. He had gotten married when he was only sixteen, and it looked as though this was one of those few young marriages to work out. He was now twenty, and all that mattered to him was to get home safely to his little family.

Anyway, seeing we were going back to Stud, I mounted the truck. And upon arriving at Stud, I made my way to the BAS. After extracting the shrapnel, they medevaced me to the rear, and from there I was sent to the Third Med where I underwent x-rays of my hand and wrist. They bandaged my hand and sent me back to the rear for two weeks of convalescence. I couldn't stand being back there with all the lifers where your combat boots had to be polished, pant legs bloused, and hat on at all times. Rather than put up with that bullshit, I decided to go back out. I could take along extra bandages and change dressings daily myself.

I caught the first chopper to Stud but was unable to get any further due to the rain. They were only to stay in the bush for five days, so I probably wouldn't be getting out there now. I met my buddies in the mess hall, and every day I would relax to the comforts of a cold beer or two. We would even see a show at night and at times go to the swimming hole to relax.

On the way to the swimming hole, which was situated between Stud and Ca Lu, we had to pass the dump. Here, the Mountgards people were digging through our waste in order that they may eat. The guys told me when they took the garbage to the bump; they were swamped before they could get the garbage off the truck. They sensed that I didn't believe them fully and invited me along on their next trip. Damn, they were right. The kids, old men, and women were running after the truck, jumping on the sides. They were held at bay by one of the guys with his rifle at ready. Like maggots, they converged on the area we were to dump the refuge at. Some were allowed to mount the truck. (This way, the marines wouldn't have to dirty their hands dumping the garbage.) and dump the waste, thus allowing them to have first pick. This is how these people were surviving. How much longer could they last?

As we were pulling away, you could see them squatting on the ground sifting through what they saw fit to throw away. If we hadn't destroyed their fields, they wouldn't be here now fighting over garbage. Man. I'm sure thankful that I'm an American and not a Vietnamese. I could hack this for a year, but for a lifetime, it would be unbearable. Too bad we couldn't concentrate our aid on humanitarian projects rather than war.

We pulled back into the mess area where I had recently met Rick Benson. He came from Minnesota, and that afternoon he had made his way to Ca Lu and brought a case of beer. It was a Friday night, and we decided to have a little party that night just to reminisce old times. Soon we were talking about our girls back home, good times we have had, and crazy things that we did. I could remember telling him about the time Paula and I went to the World Fair in New York and as we admired the work of art by Michelangelo in the Vatican Pavilion. We were struck by the work that went into making the exhibit.

Bulletproof glass was in front of the Pieta. And passing another statute of St. John the Baptist, I wondered if that too was bulletproof. I gave it a knock or two, and the bells began to ring, cops yelling to close the doors. Before we knew it, there were a ring of Pinkerton cops around the statute. Paula and I had moved off to a safe distance. The director came and inspected the masterpiece and finding that all was okay, he reopened the doors. Everyone got a charge out of it and began to relate similar incidents. The night passed peacefully, and everyone went to sleep with their illusions of grandeur.

Waking early, they told us to pack because we were pulling out going to the DMZ after all. They were supposed to be in today. I got some food from the mess hall to bring out with me, so the guys would have a treat (five five-pound cans of luncheon meat and five gallons of fruit). A Jeep came to bring us to the LZ, but seeing there were quite a few guys, they had to make two trips. Unfortunately, the Jeep got into a wreck injuring Sugar Bear, who was a big Negro fellow that used to work in the mess hall. He had complained about his ears after a mortar round impacted nearby and has been in the rear complaining since then. Now it would be his back that bothered him. He would be able to stay in the rear for some time, and when they decided to send him back to the bush, he refused and wrote his congressman and told them he wasn't getting proper medical care. He managed to get a job in the rear until his time to rotate.

While waiting for our next flight out, we built tents for our squad, so when they came in they wouldn't have to. When night came around another guy I had met, whose name was Bob and who came from New Jersey, decided to hypnotize me. I was a little reluctant at first but later gave in. I never believed it would work, but as he said, "Let yourself go. You're falling down deeper, deeper inside. You're falling down deeper, down deeper, deeper inside, spinning around. Let yourself go." After a while, I found myself doing as he said. An easy peace prevailed over me, and I never felt so relaxed in my life.

He asked if I would like a drink which I assured him I would. My favorite was Singapore Sling, I let him know. He handed me the canteen, and I told him I didn't want water. He said it was a Singapore Sling. I tasted it and let him know that they put too much sugar in it. After four good drinks, I began to feel as though I was getting drunk. I told him I had to take a whiz, but he told me I didn't. I argued, and he reassured me that I didn't have to go. And before I realized it, I hadn't the urge anymore to go.

He asked if there was any place or special day I would like to go back to. Talking about Lynne before this started, I decided I would like to go back to the day I first met her. He relaxed my mind, and it began to wonder back to the day at the CYO convention in New York City. I see this lovely girl standing in the lobby of the hotel where the convention was being held and said to a friend that I just got to meet that little woman. He informed me that she went to the same school we did, and her name was Lynne. So I went over and said hello. "Hi, Al," was her reply. Hell, how did she know my name? I invited her to a party in our room and told her I would see her later.

During the party, I asked her if she would like me to escort her to the ball, and she seemed delighted. I dressed my best and went to pick her up at her room. She opened the door and was ravishing. I felt like saying the hell with the ball, let's just stay here. No, she was too pretty. I had to let everyone else see her. It really was a lift to my ego accompanying such a lovely girl. And as everyone looked at us as we passed, I felt elated. All my friends paid us compliments, and I felt great. After the dinner, we danced and then left early, so we could be by ourselves for a while. I explained to all of those around just what we wore and what happened later. It was unreal; I was experiencing it all over again. Thanks, Bob.

We soon went to sleep; I was more content than the others because I had those memories so vivid in my mind. With the sun rising, we attempted to leave again and rejoin our buddies in the bush. Again, I got those goodies that the men would definitely enjoy, and we made our way to the LZ. The package was cumbersome, but I knew the men needed something different. They had been living on C-rats and long-rats for eight days now. How long was this operation going to last anyway? Andy was with me, and he carried my medical bag as we made our way to the bird that would take us to the DMZ. Rick promised me a cold beer when I got back, and with this we were on our way.

When the bird landed we quickly disembarked and headed down the trail passing familiar faces from the other platoons until we finally reached our guys. In front of us laid a 500-pound bomb which had failed to detonate as did many of our shells which we would pass occasionally. It appears that they have quite a few defects, as does our infamous M-16. All too often they jam at the most undesirable time, mainly in firefights when the maximum fire power is needed.

I could remember that day of August 22 when we had to piece them together, so we could have one operable weapon. Anyway, we set up our lines, and later we all would enjoy the food I had brought with me, after we cleaned the mud off it. As I was climbing down a rather steep embankment, I lost my footing and fell on my ass. It was none too graceful, and as I laughed to myself, I gathered the merchandise and kept moving.

As soon as I reached the squad, I was plagued with little things that Doc Eveland just hadn't taken care of. There was talk of getting him out of the company, peacefully of course. As soon as I got there, he medevaced himself out as an FUO. As usual, I again had the whole platoon to take care of. I made my rounds of the squads, treated their jungle rot and scratches, and medevaced another guy because his leg was badly infected. I distributed malaria tabs which weren't distributed for at least a week, and to each squad I gave them a five-pound can of meet and a gallon of fruit.

Sgt. C confronted me with a strange question, but I soon found out why. He asked if I wanted to stay with the squad or with the CP. This stemmed from the squad which told Doc Eveland to get the hell out and go to the CP. He hadn't treated them properly, so they wanted his ass right. Sgt. C, who was still waiting for his commission to come through for his actions in August, knew it was a senseless question. I said, "What the hell do you think?" With this I began walking to my squad and gave him the symbol for peace. That always blew his mind. It was also this day that I was to meet Sgt. Peraze, who was our new right guide. And before long we would be in hot water together with just about all the rest of the platoon.

Every day or so, we moved from one hilltop to the next where we would build an LZ for future operational purposes. A few days after I got there, we passed through an area where the Twenty-sixth Marines had landed, and before they had a chance to dig in, they were mortared by the gooks. It was said that they had suffered about fifty KIAs (killed in action) and about one hundred wounded. We set up in the area for a day to finish their LZ. While waiting that night, I carved "Doc Myers, Poughkeepsie, New York," into a huge tree to give testimony of my presence in their sanctuary and in hopes that perhaps someone who I know will run across it someday. We also marked "Bravo 1/9" into many trees, covering up the gook marking which conveniently showed directions through their sanctuary.

Two days before I had rejoined them, they had stumbled across a bunker city which even had signs. In one of the bunkers, Red had found an autographed picture of Ho Chi Minh, while someone else found a diary which had an entry that very same day. Within this compound, uniforms were found along with sweat shirts which had a dove with Hanoi under it. Coordinates were taken, and it would be destroyed after we had left the area.

After finishing the LZ, we moved down the trails which had been painstakingly made by the Vietnamese people who were captured in battle or kidnapped from their villages. As we proceeded upon one of the trails which had steps built into the mountain side and even had a handrail, fighting broke out up ahead.

Memories of August flashed through my mind, as I'm sure it did my comrades, as I made it up to the front to see if everyone was okay. Word soon filtered back that they had surprised two gooks sitting on the hill. Undoubtedly forward observers. Arty was called in on their escape route, and we set in. The next day, we patrolled the area and proceeded to a dangerously steep waterfall. We were ordered to descend. If anyone fell, he would hang it up. And if the gooks were around and opened up while they were down there, we could all hang it up. They would have us for sure.

As ordered, we ventured down in our best mountain-climbing fashion. Every once in a while, a rock would come loose but sparingly miss everyone. At some point, I was right in front of Taylor, who was our scout, and took care of the Vietnamese scouts who were assigned to our company. For the most part, these Vietnamese scouts were at one time NVA or VC and defected to the South Vietnamese side. I had just descended to a relatively safe part of the decline when he lost his balance and hold and came tumbling down on top of me. A small tree was behind me and stopped us from journeying further downward. When we picked ourselves up, I could see the blood streaming from his hand and quickly patched it up. We proceeded without further difficulty.

The sun, as usual, was beating down fiercely, and when we reached the bottom, we decided to take five, ten, maybe fifteen minutes for a break by the stream's edge. Some even stripped down and bathed, while others washed their clothes. But unfortunately after thirty minutes, we were again confined to the sweaty clothing and making our way back to the LZ. After getting resupplied, we would move on. The vegetation was so thick that one-hundred-fifty-foot drop-lines had to be used. Medevacs were hell, seeing they used what looked like a yellow bomb which had a T-bar for your legs and an umbrella-like top made of steel which provided protection as you ascend upward into the belly of the chopper hovering overhead.

Our water supply came in, and they were using plastic bags rather than the customary water can. Sitting on the LZ in the rear and the sun beating down on them made them susceptible to a host of bacteria. This made dysentery widespread, I being one of the victims. Lomotil, Kaopectate, Perogoric, and even Tetracycline didn't seem to be able to control you any. I could remember trying to drag myself to the next position to let them know that I was going in front of the lines to take a crap. Wanted to be sure that if they heard something, they knew I was out there and not to shoot.

Trying to hold everything back was bad enough, but the abdominal pains were excruciating. Finally, I managed to get away from the lines and just got my pants down in time. The pain was terrible, but it felt good to release some of your anguish. After about thirty minutes, I decided to get back to my position. Everything appeared to be flushed out, but I knew it wouldn't last long. Some had it so bad that they were medevaced out. They were really dehydrated, and everything just ran through them.

While walking, the burning sensation around the anus was often unbearable and foot powder was applied liberally. Some even put sand baggies in their drawers to collect the uncontrollable flushes of feces. It kept your pants clean anyway. [can't read.] The next day, we finished the new LZ, and supplies were inbound. Medical supplies and water in cans were first. The medicine was quickly distributed, and after a few days, everything was back to normal. This was the twenty-first day of our so-called five-day operation. Sure got out of hand. And tomorrow we were moving again to build yet another LZ. How many does that make? Who knows? But this is the third one since they told us this would be the last.

When morning came, we moved on, using the trails built by Ho Chi Minh followers and their prisoners. Reaching our new destination, a supply chopper came in dropping our chow in the dense jungle, making more work for us. I went along to help and managed to get away with extra cases of C-rats and a bundle of heat tabs. I had to lance Junior's arm this morning. He had such an infection he could hardly move it. Now we could make heat packs and help drain the rest. Two days and it was like new.

As the sun began to rise, we began to stir. We wanted to get this LZ done as soon as possible because it was from here that we would be leaving. Every once in a while, our work was halted when the engineers blasted some trees. The Marine Corps even had two power saws on this operation, but leave it to them, they ran short on fuel.

Sgt. C was cursing at a small tree that wouldn't fall under his ax. He had the idea that I was taking it easy and yelled, "Where the hell is Doc? Tell him to get his ass out here and patch my cut if he doesn't want to help build this LZ." Wiping the sweat from my brow, I turned around and said "Hey, pussy, what's your problem?" He smiled at seeing me working and said, "Get back to work. We've got to get this done. The old man's coming in later."

Lt. Telone was his right-hand man now after the ordeal on the twenty-second of August. He brought Dallas, his former radio man, two cold beers, one of which Dallas gave to him. He went back to the squad, told Sgt. C he worked like a girl, and then offered him a swig of beer. Taking another swig myself, I passed it on to the other guys in the squad. Sgt. C sure had changed since August. At times he was even bearable.

The next day they told us to pack up. We were leaving. We were all looking forward to it because this was the twenty-fifth day out for some of the guys. The big CP, which had just joined us, was to be the first out, and as usual we were to be the last. It was getting dark, and we knew if we were going to get out, it would have to be soon. Without further ado, choppers began arriving, taking the CP out and some of the other troops. Unfortunately, there weren't enough choppers, and we returned to our positions to wait out another night. What the hell is one more day anyway?

Again, with the break of dawn, we began to prepare ourselves for evacuation, and as three o'clock came around, we began to lose hope that we would get out today. They told us birds were inbound, but then they told us that often. About half an hour later, we were really leaving, leaving the sanctuary of the North Vietnamese. In the past twenty-six days, we had cleared numerous landing zones which would give us flexibility in the future. The birds came in, and we were headed home.

Arriving at Stud, we settled in our usual area, and I was greeted with a cold beer from my buddies in the mess hall. We had hit an air pocket while airborne, and everyone thought we were going down. Sgt. C's eyes dilated to an enormous size. All I could think of was Doc Heller who had died in a chopper crash. He was a real good friend of mine.

We attended corps school, FMS, and were stationed in Jacksonville NAS Hospital in Florida. He was accompanying a seriously wounded buddy to the hospital. The chopper took off, striking one that was about to land. For one split second, I thought the same was going to happen to me, going to die in a flaming chopper crash. The pilot assured us that all was okay. We had just hit an air pocket. Another operation was completed. How many more did I have before me? Time would tell.

October 10. Upon reaching Vandergriff, LZ Stud, we waited at the strip until the rest of our company arrived. We then had a force march to our area where our cooks had been working diligently all day preparing steaks for us. 1/9 had supplied cold beer, but only one per man. Rich had more, and it was twice as cold. The officers and lifers went to Ca Lu that night and got smashed. They even smashed up the Jeep on the way back.

At Ca Lu, they were lavished with good liquor and ice cold beer while the troops had to be content with their lone beer. We found out that the lifer in charge of supplies in the rear was selling our rations. The night went quickly after mail and packages were handed out, and as morning came, we were getting ready to go to Ca Lu ourselves but only to man lines.

I lucked out and got OP Texas which was a good mile walk up the side of the mountain. This became a familiar path during the next few days because as usual I was the only corpsman in the platoon. Every day a different squad had a patrol, but every day it was the same old doc.

Terry Landa had taken over a squad, and his was the first to pull out. We headed back toward Stud, and halfway down the road we cut in, walking ever so carefully to avoid any booby traps which may be waiting for their prey. We finally reached the Old French Road and proceeded toward the village of Ca Lu. This was a Mountayard [sic] ville. These people were forced out of the mountains and set up settlements when and wherever possible.

As we were traveling toward the village, we were passed on the road by villagers who had just returned from their daily hike to the American trash dump. From here, they scavenged every scrap of food available, as well as any item or material that they saw potential value in. I could still remember the day Lee (shortly after, he was killed when his truck hit a land mine between Quang Tri and Stud) drove us to the dump, so we could watch the gooks attack the truck in search of food our mess hall chose to discard. Now we were following these poor, wretched people to their homes.

Once we reached their village, I stood in disbelief at how people were still living in the seventeenthth century. Some children were standing, watching in bewilderment while others hid. Their bellies were distended from the lack of proper nutrients and worms. As we moved among the pigs and chickens, side-stepping in order to avoid stepping in cow dung, we finally reached the chiefs hut. While waiting, I was confronted by a man complaining of a sore throat, as far as I could tell. I used Cepacol lozenges as candy, and having some with me, I gave them to him, upon which he thanked and thanked me. Seeing this, another villager stepped forward with a child in her arms who had a rather severe infection in his leg. I sat down and began cleaning the infected site, and before long, we had a line of villagers waiting their turn.

Flagg and John were at the back road as our rear security, and Terry was with me. My supplies were soon gone, and we started heading out, so we could beat the rain. A man approached us as we were leaving with his daughter in his arms. She had a deep laceration on the sole of her foot. I sat down again and began cleaning and dressing it. The rain began to fall, and before I could look up again, I was surrounded by villagers who had unrolled a poncho and formed a canopy over my head. It would have been better to bring the girl into the BAS to have it sutured, but we had no interpreter. It was hard enough to try to tell the father to have her stay off her foot. I gave him some extra dressings, and we moved on.

As we were departing, an old man walked up to me and wrapped the poncho around my shoulders and said, "Thank you. Keep." I gave him an oriental bow and said "Thank you" and left. I would never forget that grateful look on his face, and as we were heading home, I began to talk to Terry who had a heart of gold. I proposed to start our own little operation, call it "Operation Goodwill." We would gather all the extra food and clothing, have a big sick call in the village, and distribute what we had collected.

When we got back, we presented our idea to the leuy. He was a swell guy but was easily swayed by the lifers. It turned out to be a good idea all around, and seeing we had plenty of food lying around, we could see no problems. The whole squad volunteered to carry our goodwill collection to the village whenever the date was set.

We began to collect all the extra C-rats, and we had gallons of fruits, as well as large cans of hash and corn beef we managed to get from the mess hall. As things progressed, our sergeant got interested, and we knew trouble was brewing. As things turned out, he wanted to overdo it and make it like a country fair and all-day festivities with gifts for the kids and whatnot. However, he also wanted to leave an ambush then when we left, so we could kill anyone entering or leaving the village after we departed. Shoot and then ask questions later, but dead men don't talk. Three villages were situated close together, and if a firefight did occur, some innocent people would become victims. We soon scratched "Operation Goodwill" and brought the food to the villagers on a daily basis when we went on patrols.

After about a week, Doc Eveland returned, and we would begin to alternate patrols. I sure could use the rest. Up on OP Texas, it was a peaceful day, the first one I didn't have to go on a patrol since I had been here. Everyone was sitting back manning the lines, and the others were playing Back Alley. Still other guys were cleaning up the area. Hart and Mammeral had pitched their tent on top of the hill, and when the wind changed, sparks from the burning trash set the tent on fire. The peacefulness came to an abrupt end as we began to douse the fire.

In the tent was a bag of M-79 rounds, along with the M-79 and a .45 caliber pistol with its ammunition. Heart and I tried desperately to put it out, but it was to no avail. As Heart was attempting to retrieve his wallet, which held the treasured pictures of his wife and daughter, I was trying to get the ammo out. We both failed, and as the rounds began to explode, I dragged Heart and myself back to a safe position. After all the rounds went off and the fire stopped, we began to sift through the remains with little hope of salvaging anything. We found the M-79 which was of no value. Also we found his wallet but not his prized possession. The pictures, which were his only link with home, were completely gone. He brought the weapon to the sergeant while we cleaned up. Within his bible, I found his dreams and hopes which helped to rejoin him with his family, which were so very far away.

As night fell, I was blessed with a rare gift of three bottles of Jim Beam and Old Grand Dad. From there, we proceeded to have a party, which proved to be more than we had anticipated. The party was going on full-swing when we were replenished with more of the same. They had cut our beer ration; however, all officers and lifers managed to have their fill of liquor and cold beer nightly at their club in Ca Lu, so one of our men took it upon himself to take our fair share. After all, if you don't do it, it won't get done. The result, twenty-seven quarts of liquor.

As the party picked up, so did our voices, and before long we were to get ourselves into trouble. Sgt. Perez was now our platoon sergeant, but after tonight he wouldn't be any longer. He got smashed and went out of his head, bringing our party to an abrupt end. He began smashing things around the hutch, myself included, and as I searched through my Unit 1 for some Thorazine, five guys attempted to hold him down. I had no Thorazine, so we tied him up. However, a crazy man has supernatural strength, and his bounds were broken. The only thing I could do was to notify our senior corpsman and ask him to bring some Thorazine to our pause. I told him what was wrong, and he came with the needed medication. Along with him came our new CO.

The next morning we were put on legal hold in connection with the theft of liquor from the club. We were sent to LZ Stud to await our day with CID (Criminal Investigation Department).

It appeared that you had to screw up in order to get out of the bush, and we were in our glory sitting in the rear. Along with myself were the four squad leaders, our platoon sergeant, right guide, and three fire team leaders. We enjoyed a movie almost every night, hot food and plenty of it, a fairly decent place to sleep, and above all, no humping through the bush while getting shot at. At times we thought it was all worth it, until they let us know that someone was going to jail for the theft. Then we began to sweat. Quickly we thought of a story, and everyone went along with it. We all gave the general description of an Army fellow who sold it to us and prayed they would buy it.

While at Stud, they put me to work in the BAS, and it was here I met a fellow from Alpha Company who would verify our story, at least in the eyes of the CID investigators. I promised him a medevac in the morning if he would go along with our story. We gave him two bottles which we had hidden in the mine field at Ca Lu and told him to pass it around. That night, he got pretty well wiped out, and the right people heard about it. After the CID questioned him, they let us go. We were going back to our units, and he was going to the rear. Instead of returning to my squad, they sent me to the big CP. This was my seventh month, and I should be getting out soon.

We realize that stealing the booze was not right, but it wasn't right for some lifer to sell our rations while we were in the bush either. My last operation.

It was sort of a blessing being with the command post because the higher echelon stayed away from the action for the most part. We were always protected on all sides by the other elements of our battalion, and patrols for our platoon were nonexistent, and I was glad I was with them now, seeing I was to get out of the bush soon, real soon.

While waiting at the LZ for my last operation to kick off, I was confronted by a fellow who decided to let his yellow show. He, like many others, didn't want to go to the bush, but he worked himself into such a state that he was vomiting. Compazine was administered, and I tried to console him. Then he complained of his headache, the fever before long. He had every ailment to think of. I took his temperature, normal. I took it five times before we kicked off. He lay on the ground crying like a child, and as the choppers approached, he got worse. I would like to leave him behind just because of his mental status now, but I could do permanent damage to him forever if I let him stay. On the other hand, I could bring him over the deep end if I made him go. Well, as I contemplated, the sergeant picked his ass up and threw him in the chopper. When we landed, he had a miraculous recovery.

This operation was conducted with the help, or shall I say hindrance, of the AVRNS. Our sole purpose was to form a blocking force with marines on our left and the AVRNS to the right. A column of tanks and Amtrak's were approaching us, forming the fourth side which enclosed the rectangle. Well, we thought this was how it was going to work; however, the AVRNS failed to link up. And in order to compensate for this, we were forced to pull over to our right and link up with them, which meant the others had to adjust also.

A day elapsed, and the operation proved fruitless. We had allowed the NVA time to slip by through the openings in our cordon. They had escaped, thanks to our South Vietnamese friends . . . Who were we fighting against anyway? When we finally linked up with the AVRNS, we dug in and waited for the tanks to search our area.

During the night the AVRNS fired almost continuously. At least they kept us on our toes with their sporadic firing, though it was at nothing. When morning came around, we boarded choppers, and were on our way to Step Two of the OP.

Bravo, as usual, went in first and as usual came under fire; however, it must have been the rear security of the gooks who had managed to evade us. We landed on another hill which had been secured by A Company. We took positions on the highest point of the hill, and there we spent the rest of the night. The snipers who had threatened Bravo had disappeared, and after air strikes around our position, we were ready to move out. We were moving to another position where we had stay for a few days while the other companies swept the area. On the move, we ran into heavy underbrush and rugged terrain. A rain had made the move treacherous, but no casualties were sustained.

During the move, I had managed to slip down a steep embankment sustaining numerous cuts and scratches, tearing my pants nearly off in the process. Seeing I had been taking care of, the colonel's jungle rot the past few days, he noticed my predicament. The next chopper in had a pair of pants for me. He and I got along great, and before I was to leave the bush, he would reassure me that nothing was to become of our little incident in Ca Lu.

The first day the mail had come proved very beneficial for me. I had sixteen letters waiting for me. It had been almost a week since I got my last letter. While we were on legal hold, John Swarback and I decided to write to various states requesting a state flag. We each wrote twelve letters, and I received ten before I left. Today in my mail I had one from Agnew, who at the time was governor of Maryland.

While I was gloating in my glory, especially with the letters from Lynne, a young staff sergeant came up to me. He sat down and asked if I would just talk to him. Sure. What seems to be the problem? With this he began to cry. Here, a man of twenty-six was crying, and when he handed me his letter to read, I understood why. His wife couldn't stand it any longer, so she packed up the two kids, little boy of two and the cutie of a little girl who would be four in another week. "Doc, what can I do? I really love her, and I'll do anything to get her back." I expressed my opinion, telling him that a woman needs a man around the house. She needs someone to be happy with her when she is happy, someone to comfort her when she is sad, someone to love and look after her and her children every day, not just when on leave. It's not right to make her suffer through every day wondering if you're going to make it home alive and okay. Death and injuries strike all ranks over here. The kids have the right to have their father with them when they are growing up. You belong home with them, not here in Vietnam fighting someone else's war.

Being a marine, a career man, you'll go to all the hot spots our government places us in. Is it right for her to sit home every night wondering what is next? Look how many children are fatherless since this war began. How many women are widows? Gunny Pineapple would die soon, leaving his two little pineapples home in Hawaii fatherless. They had messed up on his R&R order which would take him home for a week to see those kids and his wife. Now he is dead, got killed the week he should have been going home. This could be your fate too. Why chance it? There are plenty of opportunities on the outside, and I'm quite sure you could succeed. It's not fair to her and the kids. We'll get you back to see the chaplain, and maybe he can be instrumental in getting you temporary orders back home to straighten this thing out between you and your wife. He left on the next supply chopper. As to his fate, I never found out, but I hope all is well.

The third and final step to get under way would be taken this evening. We were going to cordon three villages with the help of the Army. We stopped at LZ Sharon, so the brass could confer with each other. While waiting, the Army was considerate enough to bring us cold drinks and water to refill our canteens. At one time, one of the Army sergeants brought over three cold beers and three cold sodas, all he had left, and gave them to our lifers, who had the gall to refuse the man's hospitality because there wasn't enough for everyone. They left them standing in the middle of the parking area telling anyone who wanted them to step forward. I wasn't a bad-ass marine, so I helped myself to one of the sodas. Pride sure makes you do some foolish things. Just about everyone else there would like to help themselves to the rest, but they were marines. Big deal. At least I wasn't thirsty. The hostility they showed the Army was uncalled for. When we got off the choppers, we had to line up, stagger packs, and stand at case, all to impress the Army. They must have thought us to be quite the asses. We couldn't even sneak a look at the USO show that was in progress.

Soon we were on the choppers again moving to the area where we would be kicking off the operation. Bravo Company was there already, and so were some elements of the 3/3. As soon as we landed, I made my way to my old company to see my buddies. The hot LZ they landed in a few days back was nothing. Everyone was okay. While there, a fellow came up to me and said, "Hi ya, Doc." Turning around, I recognized him but couldn't remember his name. He was the one I had sutured up while a patient at Cam Ranh Bay for a few months back. He refreshed my memory and said that the scars weren't big enough; otherwise, he had no complaints.

As the sun settled, we were on our way. We walked all that night through sand and then through rice paddies and streams. The going became tiresome, but we were soon in positions as dawn presented itself. The three villages were cordoned, and we dug in. A plane was flying overhead informing the villagers what was happening. Step three was in full swing. Seeing I was with the big CP, I hadn't too much to worry about. We were well protected.

That day, the ARVNs swept through the villages flushing out NVA, VC, and CV sympathizers. Some were caught burning supplies, hiding weapons, destroying documents. Some were caught hiding. Those who were hiding tried to make it through the lines and were unsuccessful for the most part, and many lost their lives while attempting to do so. Every day mail was brought out to us, and on our third day, Dr. Dick and Jim arrived, our relieving corpsmen, telling me to go in to Quang Tri for a few days. Get a few beers. Being with the big CP has its benefits and to think that the only reason I was sent there was because of the party. I might have messed up sooner if I had only known. But I doubt it because I really miss my buddies.

Anyway, I was to ride in with Dallas, get some papers for the doctor, and then return on the mail truck. When I got back to the rear, I found three guys, one who surely was to be my replacement waiting at the BAS. One was Jerry Baumgardner who was stationed with me at the Naval Hospital in Jacksonville, Florida. He wanted to see what the Nam was like, so I got him a .45, flak jacket, and helmet, and he was off with me back to the cordon. There were two other men in the truck with us, and shortly into our journey, one of the guys broke open a bottle of booze, the other lit a joint and passed it around. What a war.

Passing through the village, I threw some candy to the kids, but I never managed to have enough. We passed through quite a few villages, and Jerry was getting an eyeful of who we were fighting for in Nam. As usual, the kids lined the roadway looking for, begging for, and pleading for something, anything. Passing through one village, we noticed quite a bit of excitement ahead. There was a man's body on the roadside surrounded by the villagers. As we approached, someone opened up on us. Pushing mail bags aside, we all scrambled for some sort of protection. I wonder who killed that man. At any rate, it looked as though they were revenging his death on us. Lucky for us he was a poor shot.

When we reached the unit, I introduced Jerry to the doctor and went on the mail run to Bravo Company. The doctor just informed me that I would be leaving as soon as I got back, if I wanted to, and I did. My days in the bush had come to an end. It was November 21. Almost seven months had elapsed since I arrived, and so much has happened in that short time. I said my good-byes to everyone, told them to stop by and see me if they ever got to the rear, and I would see if I could have a few beers for them. For now, take care of yourselves. Sure am going to miss those guys. They were the greatest bunch of guys I have ever met.

Getting back that night, we ate, drank and were merry, especially me. It was somewhat of a confirmation of a flight home when you got out of the bush.

EPILOGUE

During the last few months of tour in Vietnam, Al was involved in setting up a children's hospital at Dong Ha. More than $60,000 was contributed by soldiers in Vietnam to help build the Third Marine Division Children's Hospital. The facility treated thirteen thousand youngsters for everything from minor cuts to burns to tuberculosis. Only 10 percent of the children treated at the hospital were war related. Before the Children's Hospital was built, the nearest facility was miles away; too far for many people from outlying villages to travel. Al comments, "We did some good and marvelous things while we were there. We trained Vietnamese men and women to be nurses to care for themselves after we left."

Thirty years after his return from Vietnam, Al was awarded a Silver Star for his "conspicuous gallantry and intrepidity in action" while assigned to Company B, First Battalion, Ninth Marines, Third Division. North Dakota Senator Byron Dorgan and one of his aides, Judy Steffes, were instrumental in obtaining the long overdue and well-deserved award for Myers. Al's high school buddy, Tim Schroeder (from Littleton, Co.), after reading some of Al's stories about Vietnam, could see that Al did not receive the medal that was so long overdue and contacted Senator Byron Dorgan's Office in Washington, DC.

After returning from Vietnam, Al continued his career in the medical field after being a navy corpsman by utilizing his GI Bill. He went to college and then entered Physical Therapy School in Grand Forks, North Dakota. He became one of the most sought-after Physical Therapists in Fargo because of his care for "mankind" and his compassion and his sense of humor; he loved helping people "get better."

I was fortunate to accompany my husband on a return trip to Vietnam in the year 2000. It was the most extraordinary travel I had ever been on.

This trip was important to Al. He said, "I just want to make sure the Vietnamese people are okay after we had a war over there."

First arriving in Hanoi, Al felt a little "spooked" seeing the MIGS on the runway tucked away in buildings and hearing soldiers "barking orders" in the airport—it just brought back the memories of 1968-69 to him. After leaving airport and riding to our hotel, Al felt better, seeing Vietnamese people were friendly to us.

Seeing and visiting the "Hanoi Hilton" was eerie. Just knowing what had gone on there in years past, you could almost feel the "ghosts." Also the fact that Senator John McCain had just been there visiting two weeks previous was poignant.

We who live in a world of high technology, a world where we have to struggle to make more money, where dumps flourish and where we continually strive to upgrade our homes to be bigger and more modern in order to compete.

It was good to see a land without dumps where everything is used in some way and where homes are plain and basic. The people are so much happier than we are in America, even though they have so little. Maybe the key is, "more is not better."

As I write this to finish the words written by Al so many years ago, he is now struggling with a very menacing disease, Early Onset Alzheimer's at age 57.

Al is continuing to be a very brave soldier with this as he has been all his life, grasping at memories as best he can and using his great sense of humor to cope on a day to day basis.

Alzheimer's disease is like seeing through a glass darkly, and Al is in the midst of his years of departing light.—*June Myers*

Brothers of the Wall

Though my name is not found upon your face
Our paths have crossed in a hellish place.
For us, coming home was not an easy task
Regarded by many as scum and trash.

We were termed junkies, killers and mad
Successfully stereotyped by the media.
We came home to a new war
Some to find, others to hide their identity
In a nation that ignored us
The homeland that ostracized us.

Well, brothers of the wall, please hear my plea
Make room on you granite face for me.

Our welcome home mirrored
POW's marched through the North.
We were spat upon, cursed and jeered
Forced to hold our love and hate
Anger, joys and sorrow within
Our identity as Vietnam veterans
Was better left concealed
For when we returned home
It was an unwelcome world
The real heroes turned out to be
Those who fled their duty, their country
They ignored our pain, they forgot our sacrifices.

Well, brothers of the wall, please hear my plea
Tell me, why is this happening to me?

They said we didn't belong there.
They said we all were baby killers,
That we destroyed villages and lives.
Those who were not there spoke out the loudest.
They never saw our maimed, our dead,
They never saw Bill after stepping on a mine
They never saw Al as he tried to save a friend
They never saw Bob after he lost his leg.
They never asked how it was over there.

The blood, the sweat and the tears, the rain
But they saw the media war on television nightly.

Oh, brothers of the wall speak to me
Help me find meaning in this travesty.
Help me find the will to survive.

At times, it was difficult to believe,
TV villains were survivors of Vietnam.
Even Carter would have been better on the farm.
His first official act was amnesty.
Yes, those who deserted their country, their duty
Now are welcome home
No jeers, no cursing, no spitting.
Even today they talk of a memorial for them
I ask, for what?
Because they feared death or injury?
Well, we did too
Because they knew life was easier at home?
We knew that too.
Because it was their responsibility to leave?
Well, it was our duty to stay

Well, brothers of the wall, please pray for me
Deliver me from this insanity.

The times are tough, we can't endure.
We must be among friends once more.
It was strange indeed.
America forgot we were there for liberty.
The feelings that I harbor need be explored,
The sorrow I feel must be expressed,
The joys I have should be shared,
The relationships formed should be addressed,
The sacrifices made must be extolled
Our love and dedication to our country
Should not be ignored.
Well, brothers of the wall, please hear my plea
Make room on your granite face for me,
For I must die to set me free.

The Greatest Gift—Freedom

For every drop of rain that falls
A beautiful flower blooms
For every drop of blood shed
Another's freedom is granted

We were called to war in a faraway land
This was hard for young men to grasp and
Just out of high school—what now lies ahead
A path to cherish—a path to dread

A faraway land, a goal uncertain
We were off to war in a paradise forgotten
Who was the enemy, where are our foes
Behind every tree, within every shadow

The enemy were many, the heat, the terrain
The fear, the darkness, the snakes, the booby traps
The water, the bombs, the panicked man next to you
It was hell on earth and things always uncertain

But for freedom's right, some gave it all
For the red tide of blood unshackled us all
It was our calling that freed this part of the world
A grateful people in debt to us all

The flowers bloom still, pride remains
We have secured a future in their once again peaceful land
And with every seed planted,
Vietnam grows more prosperous than before
And our bloodshed, each precious drop
Was our gift to a land
That will never forget we are all
Part of this world.
North Dakota Spring 1995

My Last Wish

No more to see the leaves turn brown, in the autumn of the year,
No more to have those good times had, while drinking a glass of beer.
Not yet to hear the young child cry, who is to be part of me and my wife.
Not yet to have the very best things that were to be part of my life.
Now I am with God I think
At least I am now calm.
I just hope my friends get home from this place called Vietnam.

Written by Al Myers

Leaving Us the Task of
Image Gatherers

The media assassinated them
Protestors betrayed them
The government abandoned them.
Family and friends shed silent tears.

We, the patriots, the survivors,
The carriers of the torch from Camelot
Must now resurrect their spirit
For the heroes of Vietnam live amongst us.

Written by Al Myers

> *If we are to live together in peace, we must come to know
> each other better.*
> —Lyndon Baines Johnson

The atrocities of war are ever-present in our news media these days, and many people are led to believe that this is how the war is being carried out. They will never comprehend how much the Americans, their sons and brothers, husbands and fathers are doing for the people of Vietnam. Some are overzealous while others can't be bothered; however, for the most part these young men are engrossed in the true hippy philosophy of the knowledge of human compassion, understanding and most important, the love of another human being.

This is practiced on a daily basis with many never realizing it. How many guys would share the last of their C-rats with a hungry Vietnamese child who could end his life the next moment? Or how many guys would have to kill or be killed, yet lay awake all night crying because he had ended someone's life? How many guys would give money in order that some child could go back to the United States for needed heart surgery while he had to stay in this war torn nation? Perhaps the money went toward a prosthetic center? How many guys would jeopardize their safety to build a school, hospital, or orphanage? But most of all, how many guys would part with some of their well deserved and hard earned combat pay in order to relieve the sufferings of his potential enemies? Well, these acts are carried out daily and to their fullest extent by most men serving in Southeast Asia.

One such humanitarian project became known as the Third Marine Division Memorial Children's Hospital, built and paid for by the men within this division and their affiliates in tribute to the brave men from the Third who fought and died while attempting to free the populace of Vietnam from the clutches of communism. A forward combat-based hospital assumed this role until a more permanent structure could be built in Quang Tri, the provincial capital. This location also afforded more protection being out of reach of the big guns hidden within the Demilitarize Zone.

"D" Med at Dong Ha assumed this role. It lies seven miles south of the DMZ and five miles inland from the Gulf of Tonkin. It is also strategically located at the crossroads of infamous routes #1 running north and south and route #9 to the west and Loas and was previously the main causality receiving and sorting facility of the Northern I Corp.

As the war spread, the people were forced to find new homes. These refugees from in or around the DMZ and areas west like Khe Sanh took up residence in new sprawling refugee's centers and villages such as Dong Ha. It is estimated that over eighty-five thousand refugees have been displaced to the eastern third of this province, now harboring under the protection of American bases. An uneasy peace prevails under this protection, and frequent mortar, rocket and artillery attacks reminded all that the enemy was never very far away.

As in the other areas of Vietnam, American medical teams have, along with treating military casualties, cared for the bulk of the Vietnamese civilian diseases, either through American Advised and Staffed (MILPHAP) provincial hospitals, Med Gap (Medical Civilian Action Programs) teams, and as ancillary services from primary casualties centers.

On September 1, 1968, Delta Medical Battalion ceased to function as the primary receiving and sorting facility for the Northern I Corp, though one ward was always to be reserved for military personnel and focused its attention on the needs of the civilian population, especially the youngsters. A team of navy physicians, including a surgeon, anesthesiologist, three general medical officers, and one of the best pediatricians along with a Medical Service Corp team and corpsmen, began manning the facility. Security was provided by marines while the Navy "Sea Bees" handled the construction and renovation to suit our growing pediatric patient population.

The first few weeks went by without too many people taking advantage of their new hospital because of the fears instilled within them by the Viet Cong. The ignorant peasants were told of the certain death of their children if they placed them in the hands of the Americans; therefore, the only patients to pass through our doors were for the most part acutely ill or those who had been injured in war connected accidents such as shrapnel wounds, vehicle accidents, or gunshot wounds. Adults with emergent disorders received emergency care at the hospital and were provided transportation to the provincial hospital or one of the Navy Hospital Ships (USS *Sanctuary* or USS *Repose*) which were lying offshore in the Gulf of Tonkin.

Local medicine care was being provided by so-called "Chinese doctors" and poorly trained nurses and mid wives, so from its onset, our hospital assumed the dual role of teaching and healing. The importance of cleanliness was accepted but not practiced, and regulations were set down but not enforced. The nurses had to be told repeatedly the importance of rules to maintain continuity in order which would help the hospital to function efficiently. At first, things were rough. Being able to communicate with one another would have been a step in the right direction, but because of our language barrier our examples and interpreters conveyed our ideas.

Though these examples, they were taught. As the days and weeks passed, our census increased steadily, and the nurses were now taking temperatures, pulses, respirations, and blood pressures themselves. By watching us, they learned to do dressing changes and debridement and marveled how we handled each individual patient. Soon they were doing the dressing changes by themselves and seemed quite satisfied with their progress. However, we kept pushing them to take more and more of the patient care and to become independent of us concerning the function of their hospital. The theory behind the hospital ran somewhat parallel to Dr. Tom Dooley's jungle hospital of Loas and all those of Medico. To start them off, we instructed the chosen few and let them carry on.

A calm efficiency settled over "D" Med as the staff of navy doctors, corpsmen and Vietnamese nurses began a concentrated effort to alleviate the disease and injuries suffered by the youngsters of Vietnam. Also, having Vietnamese nurses working with us made it appear more of a Vietnamese project, thus generating a little pride in the people who would eventually use the facilities of their hospital.

During this same period of eight months, 13,154 outpatients were seen with its primary role of practicing preventive medicine. The children were seen as outpatients in the converted triage area of the former sorting facility. Skin diseases ranked first in those illnesses seen. Contributed mostly by scabies, a mite borne chronic itching disease which, because of poor hygiene and sanitation, was usually complicated by a secondary infectious disease called impetigo. Second most common among outpatient diseases were upper respiratory illnesses, common to children throughout the world. In South Vietnam, these illnesses were aggravated by the lack of primary care, which in other areas of the world would be considered under simple home remedies. Indeed, complications generating from inadequately treated simple diseases provided considerable morbidity and mortality. Draining ear infections were first treated in some children after six to ten years of neglect.

Chronic hearing loss, meningitis, and bone infections were necessary complications of such neglect.

Pneumonia, tuberculosis, parasitic diseases, anemia, and traumatic problems such as cuts, bruises, and fractures were handled on an outpatient basis.

SICK CALL

"Chinese doctors," the local practicing medicine men, and pharmacists were our major competitors. (Culture and religious beliefs were a close second and third.) Most families consulted the local healer first, although in time we became the prime source of therapy. Herb mixtures, antibiotics, and steroid preparations with French labels were readily available to the civilians. These were administered at home under unsterile conditions, in inadequate doses, usually for the wrong diseases. This one factor made diagnosis most difficult. It was also the prime factor for death in children with meningitis, as most children arrived at our hospital partially and poorly treated already with irreversible changes.

Instead of or in addition to our therapy, their own therapies of acupuncture, cupping, skin pinching, herbal remedies, scarification and cauterization were practiced. These weren't of a major problem to us except in delay on arrival to the hospital. However, reluctance to give fluids or food and bathe during an acute illness was a major factor to morbidity.

Most Vietnamese medical personnel from physicians, nurses, and midwives, to "Chinese doctors" practice various degrees of mixed western and oriental medicine. The popular belief common among Vietnamese, especially the Montagnards (the mountain people) is to attribute disease to the entry of evil spirits into the, body. In many respects, the American doctors were a sorcerer who had more control over the evil spirits than others. Most patients entered with charms to the evil spirits, about their necks, wrists, and ankles, and petitions at home were made to the evil spirits to keep them away.

KNOWLEDGE IS PREVENTION

Popular belief interfered with necessary diagnostic procedures, mainly blood tests. Believing that the blood holds the spirits, and therefore he who draws it out has control of the spirits fate, reluctance to allow blood drawing was common. This procedure was usually done when the parent was not present, if possible. However, in most medical and surgical emergencies, we had to rely on anticipated results to prove our point of therapy.

Blood transfusions were accepted, especially in anemic children. Parents and friends would stand about watching the child "pink-up" and gain strength. Many asked for transfusions for their children when they were not clinically necessary.

A moribund newborn infant received an exchange transfusion. Nurses and interpreters watched the blood being removed and new blood injected in, in equal amounts. The procedure was lifesaving. Locally, it was explained that we had removed the evil spirits and replaced them with "good" spirits.

Even the nurses who worked side by side with us could be seen with needle marks on their forehead where they had attempted to allow the evil spirits to escape their body. After this failed, they resorted to our sick call so you can see or perhaps immange the extent the ignorant peasants go before bringing their children in to us.

Observance of holidays, such as Tet (their New Year), are a big part of their culture, and it is a common belief that if the family is under the same roof during the holiday, they will have a year of prosperity together. Well, one girl about three years of age was brought to us three day prior to Tet. Suffering from severe malnutrition and dehydration, it was certain that her stay in the hospital would be a long one. So severe was her case that the doctors were very pessimistic about her recovery. Nasal gastric tube was set in place for feedings along with intravenous feedings which would help her to sustain life. The day before Tet, her mother and brother stole her away, her chances of recovery at home were nil. Perhaps someday, these barriers with tradition and ignorance will be overcome. This will only happen with education. Then these people can better themselves, but until then, medical problems such as these with the end result of death and morbidity will continue.

The majority of the surgical admission were burned patients which paralleled a severe local refugee problem that of extremely inadequate shelter and heating. Most infants and children were burned in grass and bamboo or wooden shack like structures. Heating was provided by primitive space heating, the fuel expensive, often black market and highly combustible. This was more prevalent during the colder monsoon months, and due to weather and transportation conditions, admission was commonly delayed, and the children were secondarily infected in the majority of cases. In spite of these handicaps, of the seventy-five burn cases admitted, only three deaths were recorded over an eight-month period. An additional one hundred burn cases were treated in the outpatient clinic from January to May of 1969.

Ho Thi Thi was one such victim who had received second degree burns on her left arm and leg. After skin grafting, she had to be taught to use those extremities again. This was a tedious task, and due to the lack of equipment, we had to improvise when doing physical therapy, and though it wasn't as sophisticated as we would have liked it to be, it served its purpose well.

Don, a twelve-year-old girl HAO received extensive burns to her lower extremities and again skin grafts were a necessity and rehabilitation slow. After a few months of grafting and physical therapy, she was up and around again. Many more however, weren't this lucky. Mot for example will never use her right arm again unless she is lucky enough to be sent to the United States for surgery, and the chances of that happening are slim.

Receiving extensive burns on his chest and neck was the plight of a young lad who was known as Groovy around the hospital. Groovy was the first American word he said, so the name stayed with him. A tracheotomy was performed to ensure his breathing, and after a couple of months, he was to be discharged to home with instructions to keep his graft sites clean. Instructions were futile because in a week's time, he was back in the hospital with his grafts grossly infected. Again, the results of ignorance and unsanitary habits are evident.

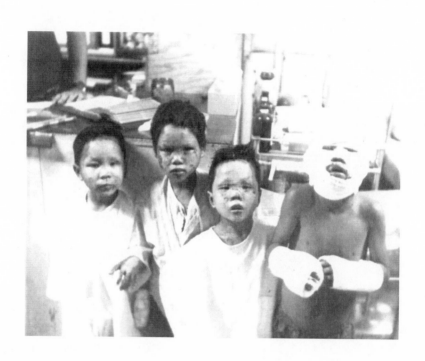

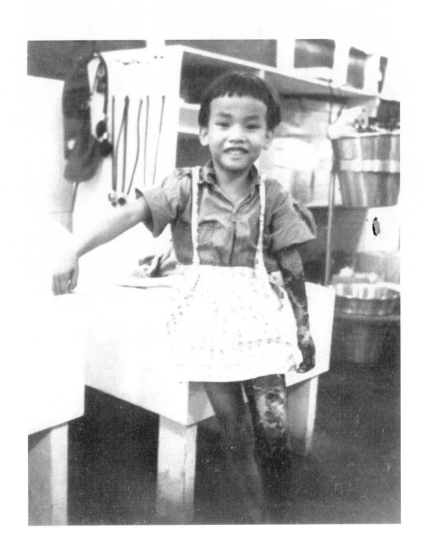

Ho THI THI—Burn Victim

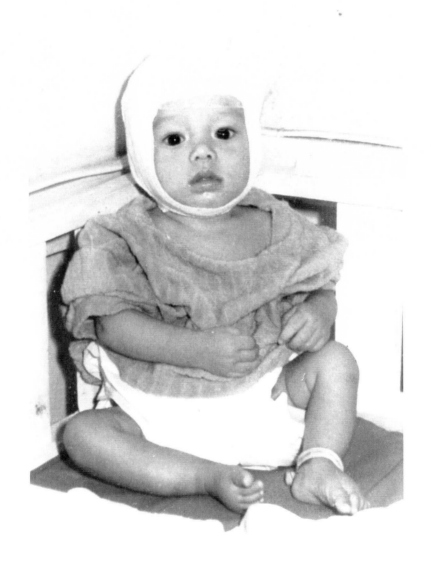

A wide variety of cases were handled at this hospital, and all proved to be interesting and challenging. Due to demand, inpatient bed capacity increased from one to one hundred in a short period of time. The total amount of admissions over an eight-month period tallied at 813, with 61 percent medical and 39 percent surgical in nature. The majority of surgical admissions were burns while bubonic and septic plague predominated among the medical admissions. Proven hostile wounds were at a minimum while additional medical admissions included severe pneumonias, malnutrition, and anemia from parasites (hookworm and roundworm), severe diarrhea with dehydration, meningitis, malaria, amebiasis, and typhoid fever. In spite of the severity of most of these diseases, most patients were virginal to past therapy and responded well to appropriate medications. Also, repair of cleft lips became an important pacification project carried out at this hospital.

Of the 813 admissions, thirty-seven deaths occurred for a rate of only 4½ percent. Many children with neurosurgical and eye problems were medevaced to one of the hospital ships lying off shore for treatment not available at the Children's Hospital.

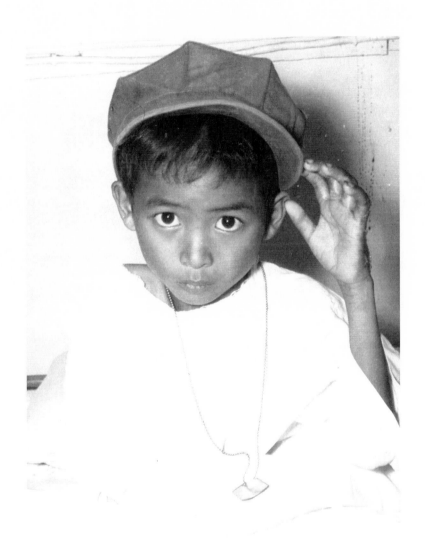

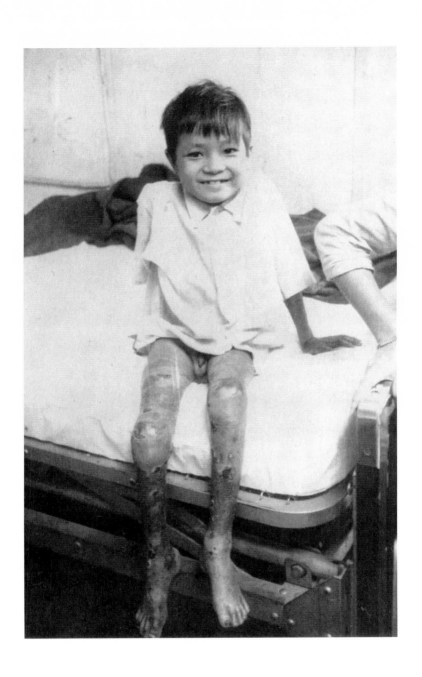

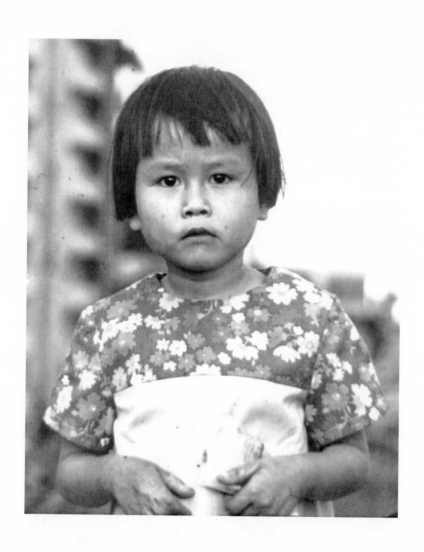

A necessary complication of burns is contractures. Even more so in those poorly treated. One child known as the "Huncho" had received burns to his foot and lower leg. This ten-month-old child had been treated at the provincial hospital, and the poor quality of nurses' training became very evident in this particular case. Bandages were wrapped loosely around his injured area, and before long there was no dressing covering the burn site on the leg and instep. After nearly two weeks with no clean dressing changes, the sites had fused together. Surgery rectified this case and many more like it.

Le Da had suffered extensive burns over most of his body, and now two years later came into our hospital to have his leg contracture repaired. In his course of recovery, he would become my Vietnamese language teacher. Sitting on his bed, we used a coloring book to get our ideas across. Opening to a picture of a bird, I would say "bird," he would repeat the word and tell the Vietnamese for the same. I would repeat "tar," and then we would go on the next picture. This became a very effective way of teaching and crossing the language barrier. It also showed that we were also interested in their language and culture as well as their health. Bringing us closer together, it also helped us to accept and appreciate one and other.

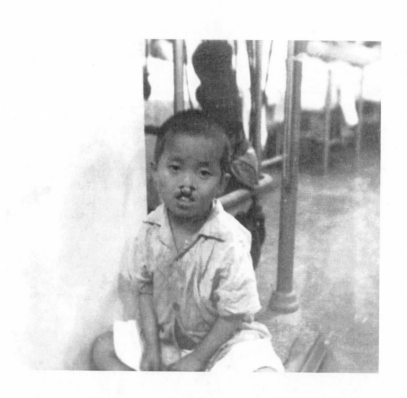

Tuong, who was better known as Pig-Pen around the hospital, was one of our first bilateral cleft lip and palette repairs. This is a before-and-after shot of this little fellow who was never seen smiling until his operation was over. Much has changed since he first arrived at the hospital as the after-shot will verify.

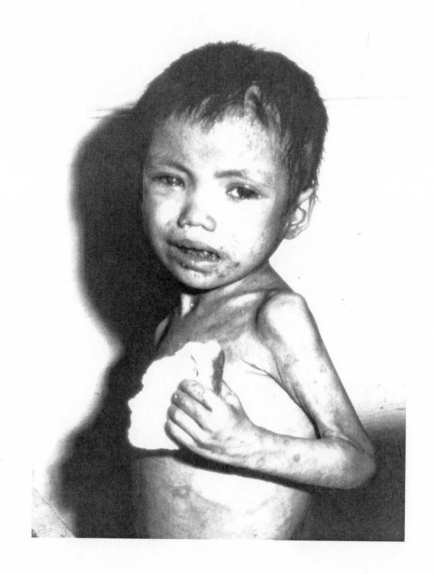

This nameless young fellow became known as Oscar around the hospital was suffering from severe malnutrition and worms. He hadn't the energy to move his jaws and eat, but after a few successful months, we would have him up and around again. To the left of the picture are worms which were expelled in his feces with the help of our medications.

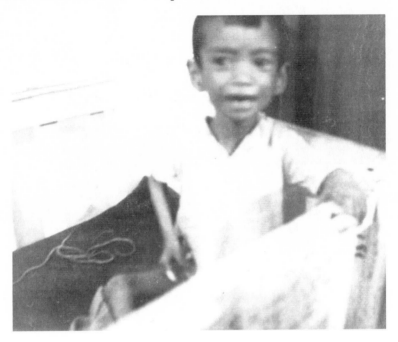

MALNUTRITION AND WORMS

Oscar, as we called one fellow who was brought to us without a name or parents, had been suffering from severe malnutrition. So bad was his condition that he hadn't the energy to cry or move. He couldn't even move his jaws to eat so intravenous feeding was begun. His abdomen was distended with parasitic worms, but with proper medication he was able to expel most of them in his feces. Getting rid of the worms put him on the right road toward his eventual recovery which turned out to be a long and trying but successful affair. His progress was quickened with extensive physical therapy, and before he was taken away from the hospital by his sister, he was walking on his own.

Cases such as Oscar made you realize just how fortunate we in America are, and rest assure if these people had a fraction of what we possess, they would be more than thankful to their gods!

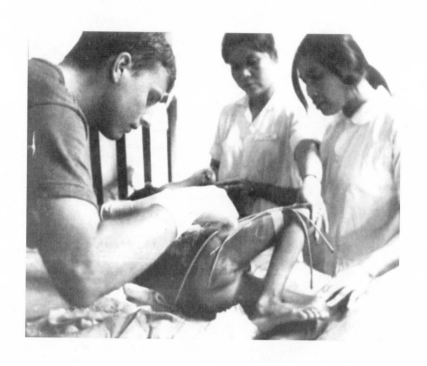

HOUNG VAN LAC

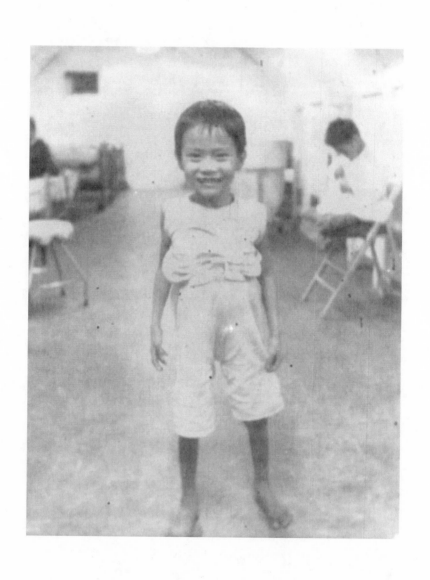

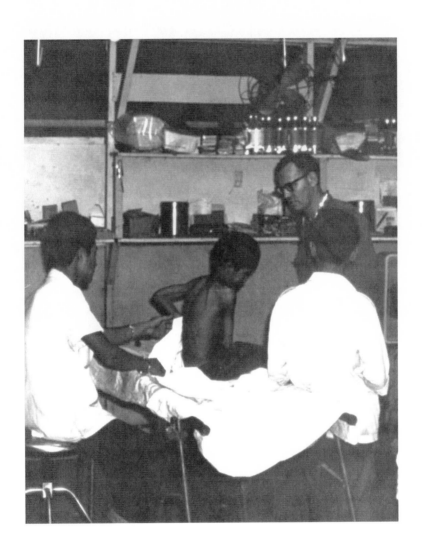

Vietnam isn't all killing, and these few pictures will show you just a few of the benefits we have given to the Vietnamese people. The youngsters of this war-plagued nation became a source of joy to all the staff and visitors of "D" Med which was located at Dong Ha in Quang Tri Province. This picture shows that these people can trust in you if you give them reason to. The little girl in my arm was burned on her leg and found comfort in the arm of an American.

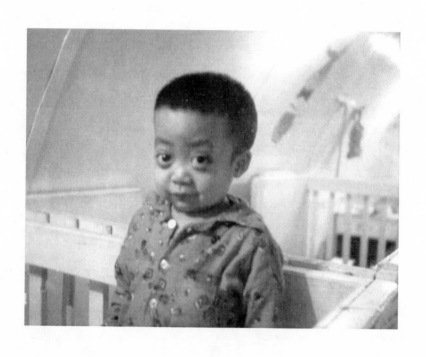

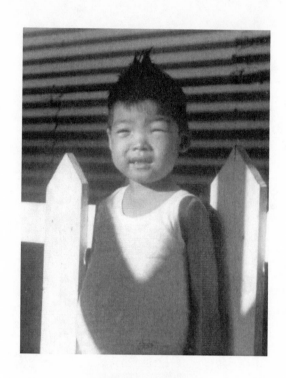

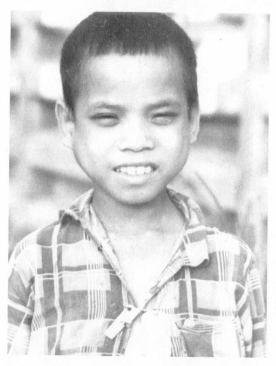

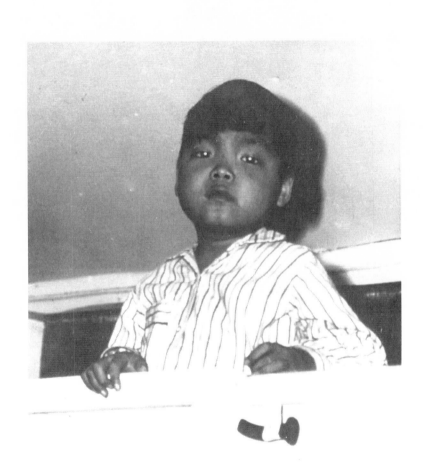

NEPHROTIC SYNDROME

The nephrotics were a particular thorn in Dr. Burkles' side. These particular patients became the root of most of the frustrations of the doctors and corpsmen who tried so diligently to alleviate the discomforts of these patients. Seeing that the hospital was filled to capacity and beyond (we often had two or three patients to a bed with stretcher on the floor.) many patients who could, would be treated as outpatients. Thao was one such patient, and his mother was given the date when to bring him back. He had enough medication to carry him through this time period, but he was brought back a month or two later.

Nephrotic Syndrome is a term applied to cases of renal disease, from whatever cause, characterized by massive edema and albuminuria. With his medication, the edema subsided, and the patient seemed cured to his mother, so he was never brought in until his case had gotten out of hand again. Medication therapy had to be started anew. The second time, he was removed from the hospital. Again, he was brought back in, and this time we made certain he would remain until a complete course of therapy had been accomplished.

He wasn't the only nephrotic we had difficulty with, and it appeared that the outward appearance of the patient led parents to believe he was cured. Eventually, we began keeping all such cases as inpatients, though it wasn't necessary, and conditions of overcrowding were prevalent.

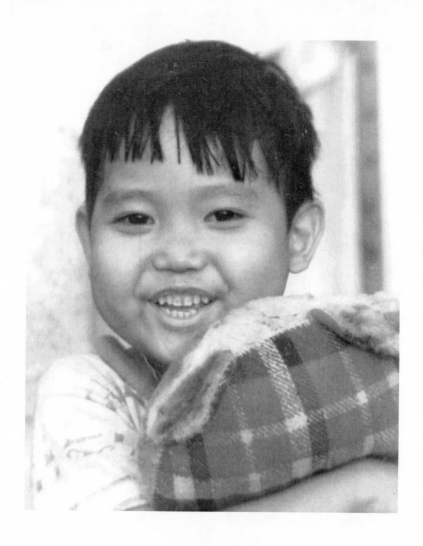

NUYGEN ANH
LEUKEMIA

Nuygen Anh was a young lad of five or six who came to us with a saber-tooth around his neck in hopes that it would frighten the evil spirits away. Leukemia would someday take its toll on him, but till then, we would do all we could to ease his misery and make him just a little happier for what was left of his young life. Toys were given to him, and he made friends easily, all of which helped him to live his last couple of years in a pleasant state of mind.

Besides the refugee problems with all the diseases it encouraged, many children suffered physically from the presents of this ugly war as in all wars before it. Some children are simply in the wrong place at the wrong time while others are the targets of immature boys who are doing a man's job. Vehicle accidents were everyday occurrences with many of them needless. Speeding by both the American and AVRN (Army of the Republic of Viet Nam) drivers caused countless injuries and deaths. Long lost his ear as a Jeep grazed his head. Another boy is now a vegetable because while he was stealing food from the back of a truck, the driver, seeing this, stepped on the gas then braked, throwing him to the pavement. Other youngsters were injured by cans being thrown off passing convoys by its passengers.

Numerous children were brought to the hospital with lacerations and many with fractured skulls due to those cans. One child was shot after his mother had told him to steal wood for their home. The sentry, thinking it was a sapor opened up, seriously wounding him. Some children were brought in after a rocket attack hit the refugee center at Cam Lo. Joe lost a leg after stepping on a land mine, and after proper healing, he will be sent to Saigon for his artificial leg. Dinh was shot in the abdomen during hostile action around his ville. He now has a colostomy which he will have to endure for life. And even here at "D" Med, it was the scene of a rocket attack which took the life of five.

The NVA (North Vietnamese Army) evidently realized that we were winning the confidence of these people, so the NVA gunners across the DMZ hit the hospital. Among the five dead were a little Blind girl and her grandfather. Several navy corpsmen, children, and three of the Vietnamese nurses were injured. Two nurses chose to leave after the incident; however, the rest decided to remain. It seemed as though the campaign by the Viet Cong to sabotage the efforts of our new hospital had failed, and our patronage was increasing on a daily basis. Our work of caring for the innocent who are injured and maimed due to the war will continue.

Injuries such as those mentioned and caring for the medical needs of these who suffer from the diseases which are prevalent in Vietnam was definitely our concern. It's truly a wonderful thing to help when you know your efforts are being appreciated. That "Thank You" look generated on the faces of these youngsters, the true suffers of war is payment enough for all hardships one could endure.

LAI
WHAT'S AHEAD

This young and attractive Vietnamese peasant girl was shot inadvertently during an allied ground operation. She is now paralyzed from the waist down. What lies ahead for this girl who used to help her father harvest rice is very uncertain. After she recovered from her surgery which included a Nephrotomy, we sent her to Saigon for braces. After a while, she returned to her ville, but life would never be the same again. The braces weren't a perfect fit because of the limited supply, so where pressure was exerted on her legs, blisters soon developed as would with an ill-fitting shoe. During a Med Cap, one of the corpsman noted open lesions and sent her back to the Children's Hospital where we helped heal the lesions, readjust, and pad her braces and then send her back to her home. Unfortunately, we could do no more for her.

Expressing a personal opinion, I would have to say that through our pacifications programs, and individual efforts only can we ever achieve peace in Southeast Asia, and even at this rate, it would take at least another five years. You can only win the confidence of people if you show that you are truly interested in their welfare. Ignorant and illiterate people are easily swayed. Former Secretary of Defense McNamara once said, "Where people are hungry and poor, they look toward any promise of a better life." Well, the communist propaganda runs on this trend. A better life for all. Indeed, we tried to make it better for the ordinary people of Vietnam; however, through inadequate administration of our aid programs, the rich got richer, and the poor got poorer. What was to be delivered to the people never reached them or ended up being sold to them. Former Marine Colonel William R. Corson goes into great depth in his brilliantly accomplished book *The Betrayal* with a devastating report of the sabotage of our other war (pacification) in Vietnam by corruption, mismanagement, and self-deception.

All of Vietnam isn't illiterate. Those that aren't have all they need, at least for the most part. The peasants in the field and their sons are the ones who will someday, if not already be Viet Cong unless we can prove to them that we are on their side. Being simple, they understand simple things. Give candy to a child, and you have a friend forever; however, if you slap him, he will always be suspicious of you and your dealings. Now the things he receives must be tangible—health, education—these will give him a chance to help himself. A chance for him to improve himself will not only benefit him but his village, his province and nation.

The presence of this hospital and others like it in definite rural areas proved to be the first link with the people, their culture, and their needs.

Pacification programs and the idea of Vietnamization of the war will someday make the people of Vietnam thankful to the United States and all its people for giving then that opportunity to help them help themselves.

Cleft lips and palate repairs accounted for a large number of patients. Leaflets were dropped from our planes over the villages in the Northern I Corp, and before long, there was a waiting line of children and adults. This defect carries a social stigma known to the world over but of a worse degree in Vietnam. One of the first patients operated on, a sixteen-year-old girl had for the better part of her life carried a cloth over the facial defect. Once repaired, she, in every sense, began a new and accepted life, the original defect hardly visible.

Tuong, who was better known as Pig-Pen (the only person who could be put in a sterile room and come out filthy) around the hospital, was our first bilateral cleft lip repair. After his operation, his father couldn't recognize him. The face that never smiled before was now continuously smiling. The results were tremendous, and once he returned to his village, he would always display the accomplishments of the American people who showed an interest in his well being. Needless to say, he would always remain grateful to us.

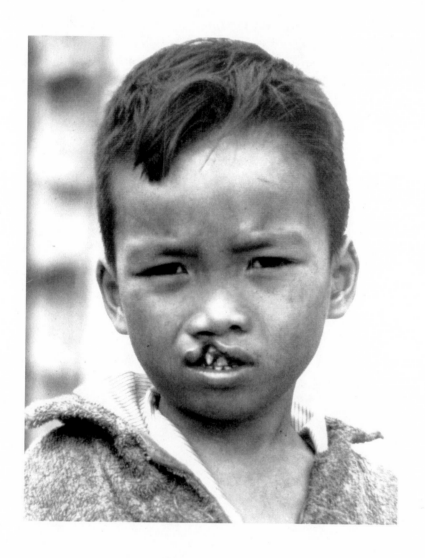

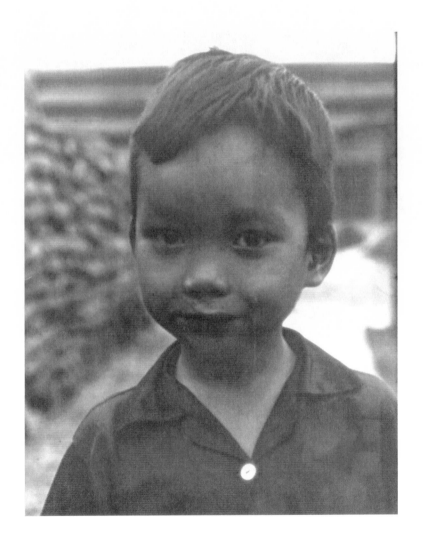

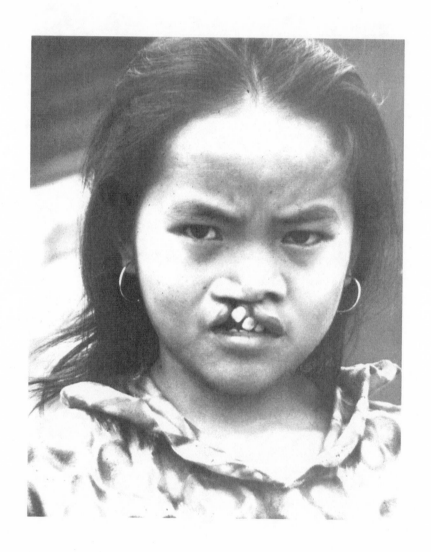

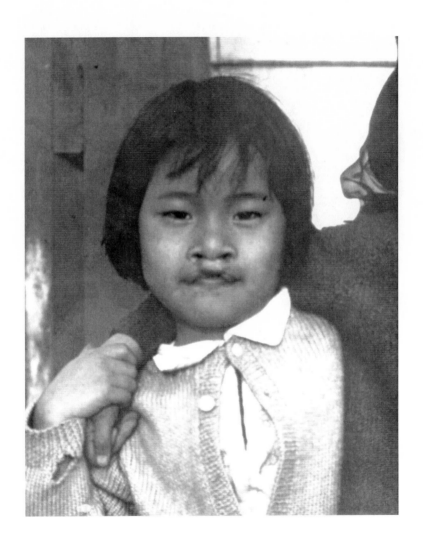

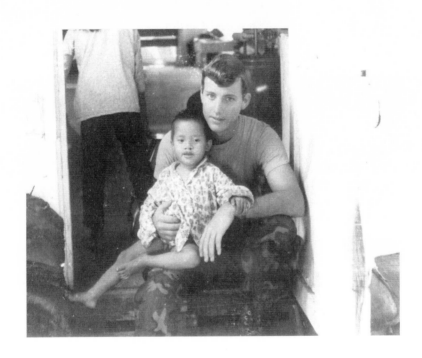

Fixed Cleft Lips

6/21/99

Al

We did what we had to do when we had to do it. And we did it well. We're both very lucky. We're both very deserving. The "Price" of our experiences is beyond comprehension. I'm very proud to know you.

Jim

A total of one hundred forty-five cases were treated, ninety-five admitted, all in severe degree of extremis. Plague, known to South Viet Nam since 1906, has become a major epidemiologic problem since 1963 and has increased in severity with the ravages of war, refugee overcrowding, and poor sanitation. The initial vector of the disease, the rat, were found dead in abundance in January of 1969 and soon after a severe epidemic developed in the northern Provinces, mainly moving along trade routes such as Routes #1 and #9 and major water ways. According to the World Health Organization, South Vietnam accounted for more than half the world's cases of plague for the second successive year in 1968 or 780 out of 1318 reported. In early 1969, Hue Provincial Hospital treated over six hundred cases, and the Third Marine Division Memorial Children's Hospital treated one hundred forty-five cases in children alone. Most cases are unrecorded throughout South Vietnam, so in actuality the problem is considerably more severe. So many plague patients passed through our doors that our preventive medicine team went to the villages to administer plague shots which helped to control this dreaded disease.

Hospital Sign
Nuygen Anh

*WELCOME TO THE THIRD MARINE DIVISION
MEMORIAL CHIDREN'S HOSPITAL*

Albert J. Myers

ABRAHAM LINCOLN.

Son of Democracy

Marines, Seabees Building Hospital, Factory In Vietnam

DONG HA, Vietnam (AP) — U.S. Marines and Navy Seabees stationed near the demilitarized zone are building a children's hospital and a noodle factory.

The hospital, a complex of 10 brick buildings nearing completion, is the No. 1 peaceful project of the 3rd Marine Division. Stringing along behind is the rare venture putting Leathernecks into the noodle business.

The division's civic action officer, Col. William E. Kerrigan of Arlington, Va., is overseeing brick production, hospital construction, customs on the noodle machinery, fund raising and such day-to-day chores at refugee resettlement, crop irrigation and the distribution of clothing, food and water.

Kerrigan expects help shortly when the "Hong Kong noodle priest" arrives. He is the Rt. Rev. John Romenello, who organized a string of noodle factories in Hong Kong to feed Chinese fleeing from Red China 19 years ago.

The colonel and the priest discussed the problem of feeding refugees while Kerrigan was on leave in Hong Kong. They agreed the noodle idea could be transplanted to Vietnam.

Hong Kong's Roman Catholic Relief Service contributed $1,200 worth of equipment for the first factory.

Space was scrounged aboard a cargo plane that delivered the equipment to Da Nang. Then a customs official ruled that the machinery would have to be shipped to Saigon for collection of import duties.

The equipment is now in a Saigon warehouse, 390 miles south of Da Nang, but work already is under way on an L-shaped brick building that will house the equipment in the resettlement village of Ha Thanh, five miles below the demilitarized zone.

When the pieces are all joined together, Kerrigan says, the factory will procure more than a ton of noodles daily for thousands of area refugees.

While the noodle factory is geared to a war-generated problem, the hospital goes beyond that.

The 3rd Division Marines last September dedicated several quonset huts in the Dong Ha Field Hospital as the 3rd Marine Division Memorial Childrens' Hospital.

Despite occasional shellings, some 12,000 children were treated there in 11 months.

This summer, Seabee-trained Vietnamese began making bricks at the new hospital site near Quang Tri City, 13 miles below the demilitarized zone, and the hospital's cement foundations were poured.

Kerrigan began a hat-passing campaign to raise $250,000 for the hospital. Of the $115,850 in cash collected so far, $99,503 was contributed by U.S. Marines, soldiers, sailors and airmen stationed in Quang Tri Province.

Christmas Day of 1968 began as a very warm day in the sense of our love for these children. The battle-hardened troops who composed the staff of the hospital put on a Nativity play, and after it was over, a helicopter delivered Santa who distributed gifts to the patients and our special guest, the children from the orphanage in Dong Ha. Those who couldn't make it to the triage area where visited by Santa at their bedsides.

As the day went by another chopper landed; however, it wasn't Santa this time. A nine-year-old boy who was tearing down a Viet Cong banner had tripped a mine, shattering both his legs. As "Silent Night" was playing in the background, the operating crew was removing what remained of his legs. The Sea Bees were good enough to modify a pushcart, in time Hung was using this to get around with. His recovery was miraculous. He wasn't expected to make it off the operating table; however, Hung, with his determination, came through better than anyone had anticipated. After a while, he would be sent to the American trained and financed prosthetic center which is being opened adjacent to the Provincial Hospital at Quang Tri.

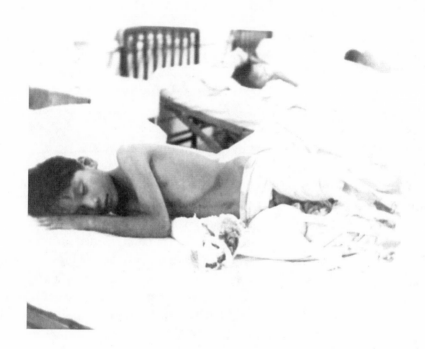

HUNG'S CHRISTMAS

This is Hung who, on Christmas day, stepped on a landmine and lost both legs. His determination to live was the only thing that brought him from the operating room. After a few months, he would be out and getting around on a modified pushcart constructed by the Sea Bees.

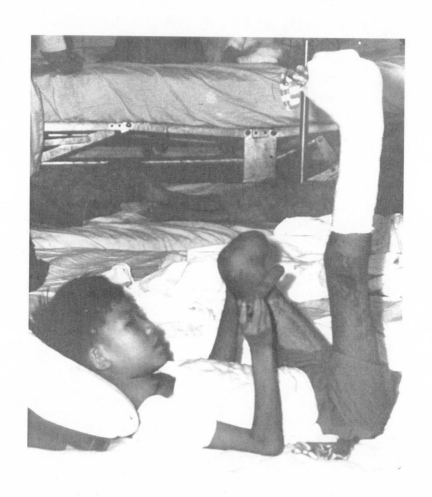

TRUONG AND THE TANK

Thanh was hit by a tank, and though his one leg was amputated, it wasn't going to keep him down. Using the parallel bars became a daily habit of his, and though he fell repeatedly, it never stopped him from getting back up and trying again.

Being scarred by a tank could be costly as it was for this young fellow who watched the tracks of the vehicle pass over both his legs. Getting out of the way of one tank caused him to run into the path of another. Stopping, he attempted to get out of its way but couldn't. One leg was almost completely severed at the scene while the other leg brought pessimistic responds from his doctors. At the children's hospital, the amputation of his right leg was completed, and his other leg went through extensive surgery. After a while, things began to look better for Truong. Through his determination, he forced himself up on crutches. Within six weeks he was using a set of parallel bars installed by the Sea Bees. Though he fell repeatedly, it never stopped him from doing what he had to do—WALK.

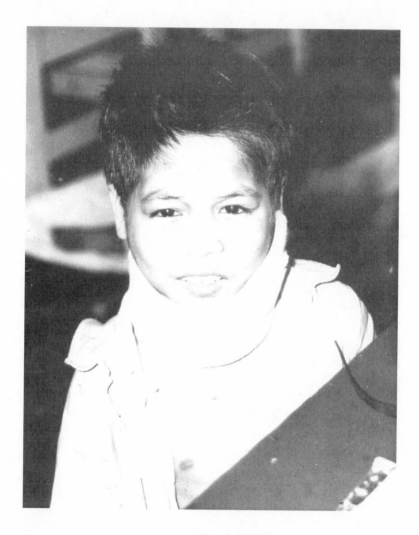

LAO POTTS DISEASE

Lao was a Montagnard and was twice taken away from our hospital. One of the Med Cap teams had spotted this young lad walking around holding his head. The corpsman had an interpreter ask why he was doing so. His reply was simple, "if I don't my head will fall off". They had him medevaced to the children's hospital. His mother would not let them draw blood or do any clinical work for that matter and soon decided to leave, with him. He was taken back to his ville on a stretcher with his head between two sandbags. As he began to determinate further, he was again brought in and again taken away. Finally, a white missionary working with these people had convinced his mother into letting us help her son. His third arrival at "D" Med was the beginning of his road to practical recovery. He was dehydrated, and his ribs could be counted under his scabies covered chest.

Potts disease is TB of the spine, and indeed without a neck brace, he could snap his neck. Lao was a very intelligent fellow and caught on quickly to the American language. Tentative plans were to send him to the United States for treatment.

Duong's father was a sergeant in the Vietnamese Army, and with the opening of the hospital, he pleaded with us to repair his son's facial defect. It would be a long process but would be worth it in the long run. He was given a before-and-after picture which he displayed proudly, and through his dealings, many sick and injured children were brought to us.

First, a plate was made for Duong, and after he got accustomed to it by wearing it, surgery was performed. The results would be envied by any surgeon back in the states, and the effect it would have on all those from his ville would be lasting.

The son of a village official, Kiet, came to us walking or should I say waddling like a duck. His legs were bent as though he had just completed step number one of a deep knee bend, and he had walked in this position as long as anyone could remember. After physical examinations, it was determined that he was suffering from Still's disease which is a form of rheumatism in juveniles. With daily medication and almost daily cast changes which helped to straighten his legs, Kiet was soon walking on crutches. One day, a helicopter came to take him home for the day. As he was helped from the chopper, his father stood nearby. Kiet tossed aside his crutches and walked to his father who was in joyous tears when he reached him.

This in turn won over the complete ville. Soon the villagers were appearing at the military doorsteps to inform us where cashed were hidden, who the VC in the area were and future plans of attack. All because someone had realized that we really wanted to help. Imagine if we could have done just one act like this a week, we could have won over most of the ville in Vietnam in the last eight years without having lost so many young Americans who lost their lives due to booby traps. These are set in place by the VC and not the NVA. These VC are probably the farmer which was passed during the day or perhaps the kid you threw that can at. We must change our attitude toward this war. Remember, its people like Kiet who will help us to make friends and gain the confidence of these people, it's not a show of strength.

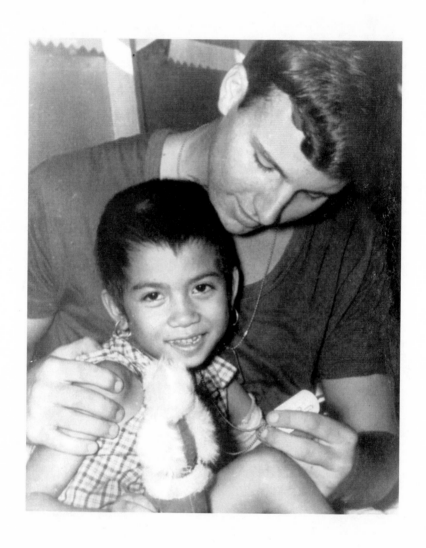

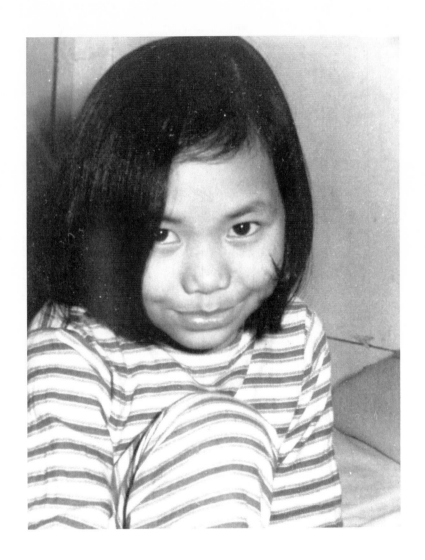

MISSION OF MERCY

Perhaps one of the noblest things done during my stay at the Third Marine Division Memorial Children's Hospital was the sending of a young girl back to the United States for needed heart surgery. This was done through the generosity of young Americans who are performing their duties in this war-torn and ravaged nation, though they could think of a million other places they would rather be. Without this surgery which was a valve replacement, she certainly would have been dead within the next five years. Others were on our waiting list, and their future lies in the hands of other Americans who are destined for Vietnam.

2 Vietnamese Children Head For States, Heart Operations

By Sgt. BOB MORRIS

QUANG TRI — An 11-year-old girl and a four-year-old boy stared with excitement as they grasped the sides of their seats while the twin-engine plane climbed skyward.

They were on the first leg of a journey that would take them to the San Diego Naval Hospital for heart surgery. Their departure marked the first concrete results of an effort by both Marine and Army units in northern I Corps to send the Vietnamese children to the States.

Navy Lts. Martin E. Glasser serving with the 3d Shore Party Bn., and Frederic M. Burkle Jr., a pediatrician with the Dong Ha Memorial Children's Hospital, were instrumental in starting the project.

Glasser discovered a heart defect in the boy, Le Hong Anh. The child's father was dead and his mother was living in a small village in the rice paddies south of Quang Tri City.

* * *

LE THI QUINT, the pretty 11-year-old daughter of a laborer in Quang Tri City, was taken to the Dong Ha Children's hospital for an examination. After extensive testing both children were found to have ventricular septal defects (a hole in the septal wall of the heart).

"We went to the 3d Marine Division's Civic Action section to see what arrangements would be necessary to send them to the states for surgery," Glasser explained, adding, "We were pressed for time as the girl was reaching the age when the defect would become difficult to correct."

NAVY SURGEON, Lt. Martin E. Glasser, of the 3d Shore Party Bn., talks to the mother of little Le Hong Anh about the boy's trip to the United States for heart surgery.

leathernecks of the division contributed nearly $1000 for the young girl.

Capt. Richard T. Murakami (Wahiawa, Hawaii) was in charge of donations from the men of the 4th Bn., 40th Artillery, an Army unit which contributed more than $1,000 for the boy.

Finally, these efforts culminated with the first big step. A Marine jeep, carrying Capt. Barry Hilton and Army 1st Lt. Allen J. Skelly arrived first at Le Thi Quit's home in Quang Tri City.

The farewell for the boy was more subdued. With the mother accompanying the small, bewildered child, they left the small village.

Little Le Hong's mother, usually a happy woman with a ready smile, sat quietly in the shelter of the jeep. The boy was asleep in his mother's arms.

Capt. Hilton explained to the mother that when the children reached Da Nang, the Rev. Gordon H. Smith, a missionary of 40-years in Vietnam with the United Welfare and Relief Services, would be waiting to accompany them to the United States.

At 4:30 in the afternoon the aircraft landed at the La Vang airstrip. Le Thi Quit, happiness at the thought of a new adventure glowing on her face, boarded the plane and was strapped in by one of the crewmen.

Minutes later the craft was airborne. It was the beginning of almost three months of waiting — waiting for two children to return home with new and more useful years added to their lives.

CROSSWORD P

ACROSS

1—Apothecary's weight (pl.)
6—Rent
11—Chairs
16—Walks across stream
21—Song-and-dance act
22—Arabian chieftains
23—Girl's name
24—Lifeless
25—Unclose (poet.)
26—Ethiopian title
28—Game
30—Small valley
32—Cooled lava
33—Man's nickname
34—Crony (colloq.)
35—Possessive pronoun
36—Manufactured
37—Tropical fruit
38—Brood of pheasants
40—Essential
42—Confederate general
43—Detest
44—Boundary
45—Born
47—Russian stockades
49—Sheet of glass
50—Sailor (colloq.)
51—Make beloved
54—Cry of Bacchanals
55—Vast horde
56—Condensation
59—Affirmative
60—French plural article
62—Angers
64—Tolls
65—Faroe Islands whirlwind
66—Symbol for rhodium
67—Dance step
69—Procrastinate
70—Await settlement
71—Vehicle
72—Macaw
74—Washings
76—Speck
77—Unruly child
78—Armed conflicts
79—Enough
82—Weirder
84—Thick
85—Piece of cutlery
86—Observe
88—Fat around kidneys
89—Stop
90—Light-colored
92—Stalwart
94—Vast
98—Damage
99—Let it stand
100—Goddess of healing
102—Move about furtively
103—Vessel's curved planking
104—Conjunction
105—Urge on
106—Underneath
108—Pigeon pea
109—Preposition
110—A continent (abbr.)
111—Winter vehicle
112—Pygmalion's statue
114—Spread for drying
116—Japanese statesman
117—Rasped
119—Containers
120—Goals
122—Began to appear to give promise
124—Uncooked
125—Short sleeps
126—Brook
128—Golf mound
129—Punctilious person
131—Drinks slowly
132—Beverage
133—Look fixedly
135—Newt
138—Free of
139—Distance measure
140—Mohammedan name
141—Anger
142—Maiden loved by Zeus
143—Paid notice
144—Piece of jewelry
145—Short, quick strokes
147—Cuts
149—Damp
150—Singing voice
152—Foreign
154—Communion plate
156—Soap plant
158—Wear away
159—Girl's name
160—Lessen
161—Repairs

DOWN

1—Moan
2—Answer
3—Haiff
4—Greek letter
5—Unit of Japanese currency
6—Emissary
7—Vie with
8—Three-toed sloths
9—Senior (abbr.)
10—Worm
11—Struck
12—Organs of
13—Skill
14—Note of scale
15—Sober
16—Abrasive instrument
17—Number
18—Note of scale
19—Flow off
20—Platform
27—Slender finial
29—Baker's products
31—Fruit drink
36—Indefinite number
37—Conflagration
39—Finishes
40—Meat of calf
41—Wash
42—Looked condescendingly
43—Cut of meat (pl.)
44—Falls behind
45—College degree (abbr.)
48—Body of water
49—Victim of violence
50—Bound
51—Brazilian wild cats
52—Late Indian leader
53—Tie up again
55—Semi-precious stones
56—Depression
57—Floats in air
58—Brief
61—Queen of the gods of Egypt
63—Century plant
67—Fright
68—Asylum
70—Sham
71—Divisions of a poem
73—Supply
74—Flying creature
75—Expel air — forcibly through nose
77—Coffins
78—Join pieces of metal
80—Baptismal basin
81—Also
83—Wheel track
84—Damp
87—Rests on the knees
89—Cured
90—Indian hemp
91—Pertaining to the moon
92—Ornamental knob
93—River in Arizona
95—Flesh
96—Join
97—Church council
99—Hurried
101—Twirl
105—Killed
106—Prohibits
107—Dam
111—Antlered animal
112—Openings
113—City in Iowa
115—Tropical fruit
116—Arrow poison
118—Dry
119—Sleeveless cloak
121—Artificial satin
123—Pronoun
125—Indian antelope
126—Undergarment
127—Sea soldier
129—Talk idly
130—One borne
131—Transgress
132—Place in line
134—Corded cloth
136—Recreation area
137—Carries
139—Mud
140—Danish measure
144—Staff
145—For shame!
146—Resort
147—Music: as written
148—Man's nickname
149—Emerged victorious
151—Negative
153—Lloyd's Register (abbr.)
155—Hebrew month
157—Pronoun

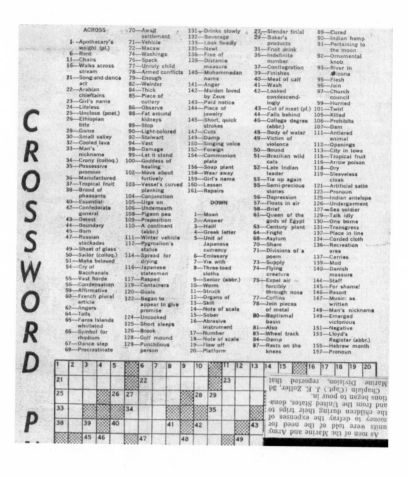

As men of the Marine and Army units were told of the need for money to defray the expenses of the children during their trips to and from the United States, donations began to pour in.

Chaplain (Capt.) J. E. Zoller, 3d Marine Division, reported that

IT'S A HAPPY ENDING WHEN SOMEONE CARES

Edwards Brothers, Inc.
Thorofare, NJ USA
June 15, 2011